NA

Words have been the tools of my trade all my working life, and they fascinate me. Certain words deserve to be celebrated in the most enjoyable way I can think of with a little laughter mixed with learning.

Hundreds of men and women have left us their names in the form of everyday words, but before we take their names in vain, let's spare them a fond thought, because, as I have discovered, the truth of the namesake behind the word can be more bizarre than any fiction. And if you haven't got a clue as to who gave their name to the frisbee, the blanket, the condom or the guppy, then the correct answers can be found at the end of this book.

Jon Pertwee

NAMESAKES

compiled by
Jon Pertwee
and
Mel Croucher

SPHERE BOOKS LIMITED

ACKNOWLEDGEMENTS

Grateful thanks to Carol Ann Wright
for her research and Robin Evans
for his illustrations.

SPHERE BOOKS LTD

Published by the Penguin Group
27 Wrights Lane, London w8 5tz, England
Viking Penguin Inc., 40 West 23rd Street, New York, New York 10010, USA
Penguin Books Australia Ltd, Ringwood, Victoria, Australia
Penguin Books Canada Ltd, 2801 John Street, Markham, Ontario, Canada l3r 1b4
Penguin Books (NZ) Ltd, 182–190 Wairau Road, Auckland 10, New Zealand

Penguin Books Ltd, Registered Offices: Harmondsworth, Middlesex, England

First published in Great Britain by Sphere Books Ltd 1988

Copyright © by Jon Pertwee and Mel Croucher 1988

Copyright © illustrations by Mel Croucher 1988

Made and printed in Great Britain by
Richard Clay Ltd, Bungay, Suffolk

CONTENTS

13 CAREERS for SCHOOL-LEAVERS

BLUEBEARD
male chauvinist pig (qv)

(a) Named after Gilles de Retz (?–1440), 'La Barbe Bleue', a sadistic French general who married seven wives, murdered six of them, but was himself slain by his seventh brother-in-law.

(b) Named after Captain 'Bluebeard' Morgan (1538–97), pirate, murderer and British governor of Jamaica. Morgan used and abused an army of female slaves, and was knighted in 1591.

(c) Named after Bluebeard, the gross adversary of Popeye the Sailor and tormentor of the strident Olive Oyle, in the American cartoon series.

BOBBY
a British police officer

(a) Named after Robert the Bruce (1317–68), who organized a band of vigilantes to protect Scottish villages against the incursions of the English.

(b) Named after Sir Robert Peel (1788–1850), Lancastrian chum of Lord Byron, inventor of the police force, who killed himself dismounting a horse.

(c) Named after Bob B Sockse (1814–97), gigantic London police chief, who was disgraced during the 'Rollmop Herrings' tragedy.

BOFFIN
experimental researcher, slightly detached from the normal

(a) Named after Mr Boffin, a peculiar gentleman whose eccentric behaviour is recorded in the tale of *Our Mutual Friend* by Charles Dickens.

(b) Named after Sir Julian 'Boffin' Barnes-Wallis (1901–84), inventor of the bouncing bomb, swing-wing jet, vertical-take-off aircraft, multi-staged rocket, and pogo-stick.

(c) Named after Megan M Boffin (1906–50), Welsh veterinarian and founder of the Women-Towards-the-Understanding-of-Fish movement. She was assassinated by herring.

HOOKER
call girl, prostitute

(a) Named after Major General Joseph 'Fighting Joe' Hooker, (1814–79). 'Fighting Joe' led Unionist troops against the Confederates during the 1862 Peninsular Campaign. To jolly things along, he imported a horse-drawn mobile brothel into the war zone, with Paris décor. The Unionists won the Civil War.

(b) Named after Millie Hooker (?–1882), the first professional whore to enter the Yukon during the heady days of the gold rush. Millie arrived with half a ton of accoutrements and a bodyguard named Henry, and established several impressive salons before retiring to Garden City, New York, a respected member of the community.

(c) Named after Arnold Coillons Hooker (1849–1920), a Milwaukee congressman. In 1914 Hooker promoted a bill which declared that soliciting by prostitutes or their

4

pimps, living off immoral earnings and the corruption of the nation's youth were all indictable offences. He succeeded in driving the industry 'underground' and made it more simple for the growing power of the mobsters to control vice in the nation's northern cities.

HOUDINI
escapologist

(a) Named after Harry Houdini (1873–1926). Originally a locksmith, Houdini became a student of psychic manifestations before gaining world fame as an entertainer. His illusions were often dangerous, and sometimes spectacular.

(b) Named after Tony Houdini (1924–52). Starting his career at the age of five when his father tried to flush him down the lavatory, Houdini progressed to leaving restaurants without paying. His probation officer became his agent in 1951, succeeding where his father had failed.

(c) Named after Alfie Houdini (1904–52). An unsuccessful burglar who became a celebrated escaper, boasting that no prison could hold him. He wrote an amusing autobiography in 1950, which summarized no less than fifteen jail breaks.

HYPNOTISM
induced method of simulating trance

(a) Named after Mesmer Hypnosus (1513–69). Hypnosus claimed to be in communication with departed spirits including Aristotle and Plato. He fled his native Aix-la-Chapelle in 1552, accused of heresy.

(b) Named after Bernado Hypnoti (1842–1909). A well-known figure of the London music halls, Hypnoti would put volunteers from the audience 'under de fluences'. His wife Hannah Malley was his most successful 'plant', a role later adopted by their daughter Edwina.

(c) Named after Hypnos, the god of sleep. In *The Iliad*, Homer states that Hypnos is capable of putting anyone into a state of deep slumber, including Zeus himself.

MESMERIST
hypnotist (qv) *manipulator of the mind*

(a) Named after Dr Anton Franz Mesmer (1837–1927), pioneer Dutch psychoanalyst. His controversial methods of freeing the subconscious caused him to emigrate to the US, where he did important research into reincarnation and race-memory.

(b) Named after Andre Balthazaar Mesmer (1830–75). French illusionist and satanist who scandalized Paris society by inducing young people to perform outrageous acts with roast chickens, while under the influence of his powers.

(c) Named after Franz Anton Mesmer (1734–1815), an Austrian physician who claimed to possess vast occult powers. He broadcast his theory of animal magnetism far and wide, before being declared a fraud by the French government in 1778.

PEELER
officer of the law

(a) Named after Sir Robert Peel (1788–1850). A wealthy Tory, Peel entered parliament by bribery and corruption. He aided Catholic rights and invented Income Tax.

(b) Named after Sir Robert Peel (1811–72). Of humble origins, Peel organized vigilante ruffians into a disciplined metropolitan law enforcement organization. He died insane.

(c) Named after Sir Robert Peel (1724–1812). British military strategist who campaigned with disastrous results in the American War of Independence. Peel grew to the height of five feet eleven inches by the age of thirteen.

PINKERTON
private detective

(a) Named after Allan Pinkerton (1819–84), a Scot who emigrated to Chicago in 1842. After organizing gangs of thugs to break strikes. Pinkerton set up the first commercial detective agency in 1850, and went on to become a national celebrity. He completed the entertaining *Thirty Years a Detective* just before his death.

(b) Named after Mabel Lucy Pinkerton, Baroness Loam (1796–1861), who engaged a small army of snoopers to record the infidelities of her husband, leading to a much publicized divorce. 'Pinkertoning' became synonymous with eavesdropping.

(c) Named after Dr Ivor Pinkerton (1819–84), a schoolmaster and early influence on Arthur Conan Doyle, who is said to have used Pinkerton's character and powers of deduction as the model for his world famous creation, Sherlock Holmes.

PRY
to interfere out of curiosity

(a) Named after Sir Leslie Pry (1814–84), Queen's Councillor and hanging judge, who organized a network of underworld informers in London.

(b) Named after King Priam, whose curiosity led to his discovery of Helen of Troy's infidelity, and led to a decade of war and bloodshed.

(c) Named after Paul Pry, the super-inquisitive central character in the farce by John Poole (1786–1872). Pry's sentences always began with, 'I hope I don't interrupt.'

RACHMANISM
exploitation of tenants by landlords

(a) Named after Milos Rachmaninov (1820–62), a Russian landowner who kept his serfs in barbaric conditions. Ironically, this blood money enabled his celebrated nephew to study music at St Petersburg.

(b) Named after Jethro Horner alias 'the Racked Man' (1720–62). Horner was rent collector for the Duke of Beaufort, and was murdered for his extortion by being torn apart on a medieval rack.

(c) Named after Peter Rachman (1920–62). A Pole living in London, Rachman used thugs to harass his tenants. His behaviour led to the 1957 Rent Act.

SANTA CLAUS
alias Father Christmas, the good child's bountiful benefactor

(a) Named after Saint Claud, patron saint of civil servants, who ordained salary increases every Christmas Eve.

(b) Named after Sinter Klaas Nicholas, Bishop of Maya, Holland, who enjoyed extracting carrots from small shoes.

(c) Named after Sanjay Glars, Thugee mystic leader, who taught his followers that irritating children must be strangled.

SHYSTER
unscrupulous professional rat

(a) Named after Mr Scheuster, an American lawyer of the 1840s. Scheuster gained success, fame and wealth by screwing everyone he came into contact with.

(b) Named after Hannibal Shyte, the loathsome money-lender in Charles Dickens' *Bleak House*.

(c) Named after Eugene Scheistrach (1862–1953), who made a fortune out of shipping European refugees to the New World, and taking all their possessions in payment, including wedding rings.

SEX...

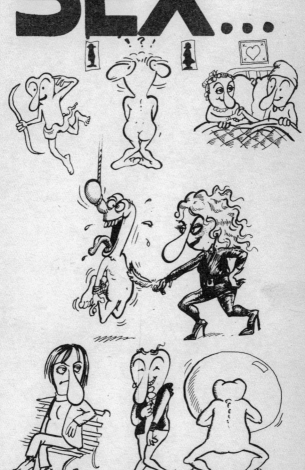

CISSY
an effeminate male

(a) Named after Cisco Kid, television cowboy of the late 1950s. Cisco dressed in style, rode side-saddle and was inseparable from his Mexican compadre. They ended each show with the words 'Oh Cisco,' 'Oh Pancho!' before the credits rolled.

(b) Named after Cedric 'Cicely' Lawrence (1919–69), the stunning female impersonator, popular at Royal Family house parties. Cicely traditionally began his act by emerging from a decorated wardrobe, and originated the catch-phrase, 'I'm coming out of the closet!'

(c) Named after Cecilia, the Tudor name for the youthful male actors who traditionally played female roles. Probably a corruption of 'sister.'

CONDOM
contraceptive sheath, subject to British Standard No 85 3704

(a) Named after Colonel Cundun. In 1665 this Colonel of the Guards fabricated an airtight oil-skin sheath rolled back on itself into a loop, for the protection and rapid insertion of the Colours of the Regiment.

(b) Named after Le Compte de Condom (1436–1513). Afraid of contracting the ubiquitous court syphilis, but unable to resist the temptations of the flesh, Condom protected his aristocratic member with wolf's teats.

(c) Named after Jas Condon (?–1763.) Little is known about this Oxford apothecary other than his advice to the young people of his day; 'If ye walk through rain, always wear a cloak.' His cone-shaped cloaks were made of two layers of fine silk.

EROTIC
that which precipitates sexual stirrings

(a) Named after Herotica, better known as King Herod. He ordered the length of cloth now called the Shroud of Turin, to be shortened to mid-calf length.

(b) Named after Eros, the god of love, whose cherubic form in Piccadilly is a mecca for pideons, pimps and carbon monoxide sniffers.

(c) Named after Montagu Erotica (1853–1919), Italian photographer and student of Daguerre, whose studies of the female form put the art into tart.

HERMAPHRODITE
body of a woman, genitalia of a man, interesting dancing partner

(a) Named after Spiros Hermaphro (1813–1905). A pioneer Anglo-Greek chef, and inventor of the gingerbread woman and toad-near-the-hole.

(b) Named after Margueritte Hermaphroditz (1782–1847). An Austrian, she was exhibited and feted in the capitals of Europe, leaving her body to science and her name to the world.

(c) Named after Hermaphroditus, a lovely fifteen year old boy. While bathing naked in a spring, he was passionately leaped on by Salmacis the water nymph. Such was her lust that their bodies fused into one.

LESBIAN
woman who prefers sexual relationships with other women

(a) Named after Sappho, alias Lesbos, a Greek poetess of the sixteenth century B C. She was exiled to Sicily, where she wrote passionate and erotic poetry of love for several women.

(b) Named after Morag Cindy Lesbian (1852–78), founder member of the Streatham Women's Male-voiced Choir. Morag was witty, very beautiful and extremely intelligent, and she lived for several years under the assumed name of Albert Poove.

(c) Named after Lesbiana, Greek goddess of the trees, who, disguised as a unicorn, seduced Diana the Huntress.

MASOCHISM
self-infliction of pain and humiliation, often sexually perverted

(a) Named after Leopold von Sacher-Masoch (?–1895), an Austrian novelist. Sacher-Masoch appeared in an 1893 medical dictionary for his pains.

(b) Named after Masochius (132–84 B C), a Roman centurian who every Ides bathed in wasps.

(c) Named after Hernia Masochist (1939–), who is the founder of the Dusseldorf Chapter of the James Last Orchestra Appreciation Society.

PLATONIC LOVE
spiritual or intellectual love, devoid of sexuality

(a) Named after Manitas de Plata (1917–), the famous gypsy flamenco guitarist, who married his second best guitar in 1942, and took it to America as a war bride.

(b) Named after Plato (?–347 BC), the greatest of the Greek thinkers, idealist philosopher, who conceived of the Music of the Heavenly Spheres.

(c) Named after Platon, Greek god of celibacy, whose followers developed remarkable achievements in the science of cold-shower construction.

PUFF
effeminate man

(a) Named after Georgina Pufton (1782–1826) who, as George Pufton, was elected Whig member of parliament for Leamington in 1823. She never took her seat, failing the rigorous 'Members' Test' of pederast Black Rod.

(b) Named after Mr Puff, who sprang from the pages of Sheridan's play *The Critic* when the author was locked in his room for two days with nothing but bottles of claret for sustenance. When not declaring his love for a young boy, Mr Puff applauded everything.

(c) Named after Puff, the magic dragon, in Dorothy Keatle's weird children's book. Puff led little Jacky Paper astray, making him perform bizarre acts with toadstools. The book was suppressed after publication, but the characters reappeared in a tongue-in-cheek folk-song by Peter, Paul and Mary.

SADISM
sexual perversions utilising mental and physical cruelty and pain

(a) Named after Sadie Thompson (?–1897), who chopped up her parents with a hatchet, during an argument over lace. She captured the investigating sheriff and subjected him to bonded rape, before making him into pasties.

(b) Named after Donatien Alphonse François, Marquis de Sade (1740–1814). At the age of thirty-two he was sentenced to death for sexual vices perpetrated against several persons. De Sade escaped but was recaptured and sent to Vincennes and later the Bastille, where he executed several works. The Marquis died insane at Charenton.

(c) Named after Sir Mark Edith Sade (1842–1930), who was at the centre of the notorious 'Inverness Scandal' of 1921, involving Adolph Sax, (qv) four boy scouts and a squid.

TANTALIZE
to tease or to frustrate

(a) Named after Tantular, the mythological Greek spider god, in whose huge web Jason and the Argonauts were entrapped within reach of three vestal virgins, two camels and a melon.

(b) Named after Tantalus, the Greek king, and father of Penelope. Tantalus was a very naughty king, and was punished in Hades by having to stand up to his knees in water that receded when he bent down to drink it, and under fresh fruit that self-elevated as he tried to reach and grab it. Tantalus suffered from a bad back.

(c) Named after Henry Irving Tantalus (1749–1812), as a foil against his dipsomaniac manservant, George Pissaro. The Tantalus was a lockable booze cabinet, that revealed the contents of its bottles, whilst securing their stoppers in a halter.

...AND VIOLENCE

BIG BERTHA

142 ton German cannon which shelled Paris in 1918 from a distance of seventy-six miles

(a) Named after Bertha Krupp von Bohlen und Halbach (1866–1957), who inherited the Krupp armaments factory from her suicidal father. Bertha was built like a concrete blockhouse, made two fortunes from the mass deaths of both world wars, and died peacefully in her bed.

(b) Named after Bertha D Blews (1869–1918), American gospel singer and daughter of a slave, who travelled to Flanders in 1917 to entertain the troops.

(c) Named after Bertha Boogerov (1840–1929), Olympic weight-lifting champion who modelled for the hull of the Titanic.

BOWIE

knife with a curved blade

(a) Named after Colonel Jim Bowie (1790–1836), folk hero, partner of Davy Crockett and injun-fighter. He met his death in the Texas war.

(b) Named after David Bowie (1945–   ), gaunt actor and singer, who employs such a knife to trim his hair and to pick his finely stained teeth.

(c) Named after Charles Beau-Isle (1653–1726), French surgical instrument maker, whose annealed blades advanced medical science during the Codpiece War against Sardinians.

COLT 45
'revolver' type handgun

(a) Named after William 'Buffalo Bill' Colt (1814–1901), hero of the Wild West, showman and charlatan, on the occasion of his forty-fifth birthday.

(b) Named after Samuel Colt (1814–62), a Connecticut inventor, who took out a patent for a rotating breach pistol in 1835, and promptly won a contract of 1,000 revolvers for the US army.

(c) Named after 'Kid Colt', alias Lambert Grierson (?– 1877), hired gun and bounty hunter who allegedly killed forty-five very tall men and lived on chocolate bars filled with coconut.

DERRINGER
short-barrelled large-bore pocket-pistol

(a) Named after Hugh Whanquer Derringe (1869–1901), Liberal MP for Keswick, who shot himself in the foot, usually on Tuesdays.

(b) Named after Henry Deringer (1786–1869), a Philadelphia gunsmith who was responsible for making the weapon that assassinated Abraham Lincoln.

(c) Named after Ferdinand de Ringers (1701–86), captain of musketeers to Louis XIV. His minute hand-guns were exquisitely crafted, often using precious metals and jewels.

DRACONIAN
unreasonably severe punishment

(a) Named after Draco, the Athenian leader, who decreed in 621 BC that urinating in public was punishable by death.

(b) Named after Fredo Draconi (1871–1942), fascist Justice Supremo under Mussolini, who decreed that singing 'The Internationale' in public was punishable by death.

(c) Named after Dracula, the vampire of Bram Stoker's novel, who never sang or urinated in public.

GAT
slang expression for a gun, derived from Gatling gun

(a) Named after Richard Jordan Gatling (1818–1903). Gatling was a fully qualified medical doctor, who never once practised medicine. He built his machine-gun in 1862, and although it was not particularly accurate, it sounded impressive.

(b) Named after Thomas Boone Gatling (1798–1884), the inventor of nitroglycerine in 1857, the pin-release hand grenade in 1869, and the multi-barrelled artillery machine-gun in 1881.

(c) Named after Caesare 'Gato Gordo' Gatling (1887–1926), Detroit gangster, who had fitted to his forearm a spring-powered automatic pistol, which travelled along a rail at great speed from his sleeve to his hand. Gatling disappeared during the internecine mob war known as Ice Cream Sunday.

GUILLOTINE
device for chopping off heads, popular in France

(a) Named after Honoré Eugene Guillotine (1717–96). The Guillotine works at Rouen used the finest steel for decorative cigar cutters and industrial paper cutters. Guillotine was ordered to supply the revolutionary government with blades for their first mass executions.

(b) Named after Joseph le Compte de Guillotine (1736–1814). A thoroughly bad egg; cruel, vindictive and miserly. He advocated beheading for stealing currant buns, utilizing his machine in 1768 for the first time. He was himself guillotined by the mob, six weeks after the storming of the Bastille.

(c) Named after Joseph Ignace Guillotine (1738–1814), a French physician and humanitarian, who detested unnecessary violence. He advocated a quick and painless method of execution, his prototype being constructed in 1792 by a German mechanic named Schmidt.

HOOLIGAN
unruly youth

(a) Named after Patrick Hooligan, robber and thug, who controlled a gang of evil little boys based at The Lamb and Flag pub in Southwark, London. His rotten empire was chronicled in *The Hooligan Nights* by Clarence Rook in 1899.

(b) Named after Sebiohan Hoolihan (1685–1754), who demolished an ale house, two handcarts and a smithy, during the Puck Fair of 1745, while looking for her Uncle Toby.

(c) Named after Bernard Hooligh (1813–1900). At the age of nineteen, Mr Hooligh said 'bum' to Mrs Radcliffe of 64 Meadowvale Green, Stevenage, Hertfordshire.

JACK JOHNSON
5.9 German howitzer of the First World War, making a loud bang and dense black smoke

(a) Named after Sgt John Johnson (1876–1927). In 1916 Johnson saved the lives of twenty men under his command, by knocking out a German gunnery position which had pinned them down. He was awarded the Victoria Cross.

(b) Named after Jacob Johanson (1860–1920), the Swedish inventor of this piece of artillery, which was offered for sale to the Kaiser's army only after the British had rejected it for being inaccurate.

(c) Named after Jack Johnson (1878–?), the heavy-weight boxing champion of the world from 1908–15. The unfortunate man was sentenced to long-term imprisonment in 1919, and died in obscurity.

LEWIS GUN
automatic weapon

(a) Named after Marco Polo Lewis (1858–1931). An Australian engineer, and the inventor of this gun in 1927, electric sheep shears in 1925 and an automatically operated caustic bath.

(b) Named after Isaac Newton Lewis (1858–1931). An American army officer, and the inventor of this machine-gun in 1911, an artillery range-finder and a fire-control system.

(c) Named after Horatio Nelson Lewis (1858–1931). A Welsh militarist, who invented his gun in 1896, and first fitted a telescopic sight to a rifle, a .303, in 1912.

LYNCH LAW
on-the-spot rough justice

(a) Named after Charles Lynch, (1736–96), an American Justice of the Peace. In 1780 he imprisoned a gang of men for conspiracy, thereby exceeding the limits of his authority.

(b) Named after James Lynch Fitzstephen, the Mayor of Galway. To prove that under his authority no crime would go unpunished, Lynch hanged his own son from the castle walls.

(c) Named after Warren Lynch, Grand Wizard of the Ku Klux Klan (1851–1924). Lynch and his group of evangelical murderers were responsible for the mutilation and hanging of over forty negroes in and around Alabama.

MAUSER
German army issue rifle and pistol

(a) Named after Peter Paul Mauser (1838–1914) and his brother Wilhelm Mauser (1834–82), whose weaponry was adopted by the German army in 1871.

(b) Named after Mickey Mouse (1928–   ) a great favourite with Hitler and his pals, who named their guns after the little rodent in 1933.

(c) Named after Affenarsch Mauser (1869–1919), a bitter, twisted Lutheran, who hated wood-lice, and devoted his life to shooting them. His gun was adopted by the German army in 1914.

MILLS BOMB
hand-launched grenade

(a) Named after Gladys 'Missus' Mills (1921–78), popular overweight pianist, who tickled the ivories with hands like bunches of sausages.

(b) Named after Sir William Mills (1856–1932), a pioneer metallurgist, who undertook valuable research into alloys when he was not perfecting lethal weapons.

(c) Named after Freddie Mills (1919–59), well-liked British boxer and sporting personality, who died tragically after a thwarted career.

MOLOTOV COCKTAIL
home-made petrol bomb or hand grenade

(a) Named after Count Molotov Gregoravitch (1890–1985), head barman at the Waldorf Astoria, New York for half a century. His only weakness was to hurl bottles of vodka at Republicans.

(b) Named after Vyacheslar Mikhailovich Skriabin, alias Molotov 'the Hammer' (1890–   ), founder of *Pravda*, a Bolshevik at the age of sixteen with Lenin, succeeded as Soviet chairman by Stalin, disgraced by Krushchev, expelled by Brezhnev, and outlived them all.

(c) Named after Igor Tatumyak Molotov (1885–1965), world famous escapologist and circus fire-eater, who could drink and pass neat petroleum.

PYRRHIC VICTORY
a war in which the victor's losses are as great as the vanquished

(a) Named after Admiral Sir David Pyrrie (1891–1970), respected campaigner against nuclear weapons who coined the acronym MAD or Mutually Assured Destruction.

(b) Named after Pyrrik Lutyorvik (AD?–257), alias 'Yellowbeard'. A Viking chieftain, Pyrrik believed that suicide squads used to gain military advantage would be rewarded in Valhalla. He was decapitated by a non-believer.

(c) Named after King Pyrrhus (319–272 BC), jealous relative of Alexander the Great. Pyrrhus decided to conquer the world, and destroyed his entire nation in the process.

SHRAPNEL
wickedly explosive projectile

(a) Named after Admiral Otto Ludendorf von Shrapnel (1853–1919), Commander of the Eastern Imperial Grand Fleet, who based his shell on experience gained from grouse shooting in Scotland. Serious losses were inflicted on British aircraft during the First World War.

(b) Named after Ivor 'Jaws' Shrapnel (1853–1919), a celebrated freak who travelled with the Barnum Circus. Shrapnel ate bottles and razor blades, spitting fragments at his wide-eyed audiences.

(c) Named after Major General Henry Shrapnel (1761–1842), the instigator of numerous artillery inventions. His explosive shell was first used in 1804, and is said to have been a decisive factor at the Battle of Waterloo.

TOMMY GUN
small machine gun

(a) Named after Tom Cribb (1840–1903), British heavy-weight boxer, who specialized in rapid bursts of left-handed blows, followed by a right hook.

(b) Named after 'Tommy', the universal nickname for the British infantryman.

(c) Named after J T Thompson (1860–1940), of the US Army. The Thompson sub-machine gun was short and compact, and very popular with Chicago gangsters.

ALL THINGS BRIGHT AND BEAUTIFUL, ALL CREATURES GREAT AND SMALL

BEGONIA
waxy flowering plant

(a) Named after Begon Ronay (1933–), restaurant free-loader, who whilst assessing the merits of the Happy Eater, Swansea, preferred to eat the pot plants than the meal.

(b) Named after Michel Begon (1638–1710), by a grovelling toady to curry favour with Begon, who was Administrator to the French West Indies and famous for his gifts of money to mad scientists.

(c) Named after Winifred Begoni (1872–1926), children's writer, who created the Wee Winkle family of tiny dormice who inhabited a fantasy village where the houses were all flowers.

DAHLIA
colourful tuberous rooted flower

(a) Named after Andreus Dahl (?–1789), celebrated Swedish botanist. The brightly coloured, shaggy bloom resembled Dahl's hair, which he never combed.

(b) Named after Dahlia Thompson (1806–88), in honour of her successful crossing of the Atlantic in a flower pot.

(c) Named after the Dalai Lama, spiritual leader of Tibet, whose coloured robes are the same shade as the flower.

FLORA and FAUNA
vegetation and wildlife of the world

(a) Named after Flora and Fauna, the gossiping charladies portrayed by Elsie and Doris Waters. During the Second World War their comic radio broadcasts were used to urge the British housewife to save meat and grow vegetables.

(b) Named after Bona Dea, alias Flora, the goddess of women and wife of Faunus. She held influence over all crops as well as flocks of animals. And named after Flora, the Roman goddess of fertility and all flowering plants.

(c) Named after Flora, the Greek goddess of artificially flavoured and coloured soft margarine, and Fauna, the goddess of catering.

FUSCHIA
beautifully decorative shrub

(a) Named after Don Ghiva Fuchs, the incompetent gardener in Verdi's *El Son La Vatori*.

(b) Named after Leonhard Fuchs (1510–66), the intrepid German cross-fertilizing botanist.

(c) Named after Fuschia, one of the fairies in Shakespeare's *A Midsummer Night's Dream*. She is traditionally clothed in leaves with a coloured mob-cap.

GARDENIA
evergreen shrub with white flowers

(a) Named after Alexander Garden (1730–91), Scottish American gigolo, who discovered the conger eel.

(b) Named after Carmen Tudor Gardenia Maude (1599–1667), a wealthy Huguenot socialite, whose funeral was marked by her exquisite flowered head-dress. Unfortunately her face had turned bright green.

(c) Named after Graham Garden (1940–), comic and actor, who first introduced the shrub to Channel 4.

GUPPY
tiny colourful tropical fish

(a) Named after Henry Blardworthy, alias Guppy (1882–1949). Yorkshire music hall comedian, Guppy wore a rainbow-coloured suit on stage, and is said to have greatly influenced Max Miller.

(b) Named after R J Lechmere Guppy in 1868, President of the Scientific Association of Trinidad, and dwarf fish fancier.

(c) Named after Giuseppi 'Guppy' Lombardo (1871–1938), sent to the electric chair for multiple murder. Lombardo waited on Death Row for six years, breeding tropical fish.

IRIS
a spring flower

(a) Named after Iris Murdoch (1935–), Irish writer and individualist, by the president of the Royal Horticultural Society, at the 1961 Chelsea Flower Show.

(b) Named after Iris, the female messenger of the gods, who appeared as a rainbow in the heavens while on her postal rounds.

(c) Named after Iris Tew, the Chinese god of the wok, and spirit of the green salad.

JACK RUSSELL
small sporting terrier dog

(a) Named after Jack Russell (1794–1883), the Oxford educated clergyman and master of foxhounds. He first bred his terriers in the West Country.

(b) Named after Jack Russell (1695–1783) the landlord of the famous Dog and Duck Inn, Whitechapel. He pioneered the cruel sport of underwater duck baiting.

(c) Named after John Bull (1595–1683), a small sporting man prone to entering rabbit's holes.

JUMBO
elephant's nickname

(a) Named after Djambo, the Masai elephant god. Wise and benign, Djambo would be left offerings of food and drink, even when the tribe itself was starving.

(b) Named after Jumbo (1941), the endearing baby elephant in Walt Disney's cartoon of the same name. Jumbo discovered that he could fly by using his enormous magical ears.

(c) Named after Jumbo (?–1885). Weighing over six tons, Jumbo the elephant was sold to Barnum's Circus by the London Zoo in 1882. He was killed three years later by a railway engine.

LOBELIA
herbaceous plant

(a) Named after Lobelia Merdemanger (1687–1754), cur-
vaceous pouting courtesan at the court of the Sun King,
who could flatten an aristocrat at ten paces with the
overwhelming stink of her perfume.

(b) Named after Lobelia, Shakespeare's insane heroine in
Hamlet.

(c) Named after Matthias de Lobel (1538–1616), green-
fingered botanist to James I of England and VI of
Scotland.

MAGPIE
raucous voiced black, blue and white bird

(a) Named after Margaret Thatcher (1820–87), the
raucous-voiced executioner at Holloway Prison, who
sang patriotic songs as she went about her business.

(b) Named after Vieille Margot, a twelfth century French
busybody. Folk mythology has it that she never stopped
talking, even whilst asleep. She was known in English
as 'maggot'.

(c) Named after Mag, the name of the semi-mythical Pied
Piper of Hamelin, or Hamlin. In the original story,
Mag dressed in blue and black with a white sash, and
charmed both rats and children with his cackling
laugh.

NARCISSUS
narcotic flower

(a) Named after Narcissus, the mythological Greek youth who fell in love with his own reflection, and was changed into a flower by Aphrodite, as a punishment for self-centredness.

(b) Named after Maximus Narcissus (?–12 BC) a Roman apothecary, who concocted a potion brewed from these plants as a primitive tranquillizer for Augustus Caesar.

(c) Named after Lucinda Narciss (1814–97), the Shropshire horticulturalist who travelled the Himalayas alone except for her bicycle, in search of new species.

POINSETTIA
the Easter Flower or Mexican flame-leaf

(a) Named after J R Poinsett in 1836. Poinsett was a trained botanist and career politician who discovered the plant in Mexico during his appointment as the American Minister.

(b) Named after Ewing Poinsett in 1936. Poinsett was a Texan prospector who refused to drill for oil at a wildcat site in order to save the flowers growing there.

(c) Named after Le Compte de Poinse in 1736. A French explorer and soldier, Poinse discovered the plants on Easter day, and ate them with a dash of lemon and a hint of garlic.

PYTHON
constricting snake

(a) Named after Python, the repulsive dragon who lived at Delphi. Python was slaughtered by Apollo, who established his oracle on the spot.

(b) Named after Syphon T Python (1870–1905), a boorish Australasian wrestler who flouted the Graeco-Roman rulings of conventional sport, and squeezed his opponents into submission.

(c) Named after Montagu Pyth (1789–1870), the Scottish naturalist and vivisector. Pyth produced the first maps of the Brazilian coastline and the Amazon Basin during his 1840–2 expedition, and became President of the Royal Society in 1861.

WISTERIA
lilac or blue flowered climbing bush native to North America, China and Japan

(a) Named after Caspar Wistar (?–1818), an American anatomist, to celebrate his death.

(b) Named after Gaspar Wister (1818–1915), a Dutch accordionist, to celebrate his wedding.

(c) Named after Jasper Wister (1818–?), an Australian archivist, to celebrate his gall bladder operation.

ZINNIA
flower of the aster family

(a) Named after Cardinal Xerxes Zinnia (1821–94), who was mildly insane in as much as he thought Saint Peter lived in a tree in his garden. In fact Saint Peter lived in the greenhouse.

(b) Named after Madame Zin, the *femme fatale* in the Charlie Chan movies, who wore the flowers in her hair.

(c) Named after Johann Gottfried Zinn (1727–59), professor of medicine and publisher of the first book on the anatomy of the eye. Dying so young, the poets named the flower after him for 'blooming brightly but falling at the first frost'.

16 INTERESTING DINNER GUESTS

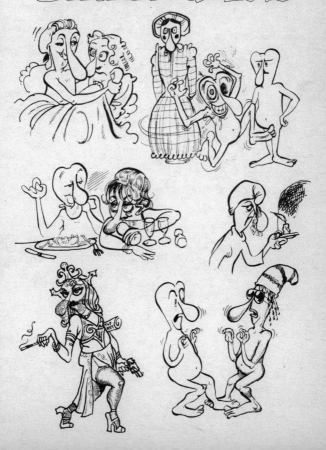

AUNT SALLY
a target for public ridicule or brickbats

(a) Named after Sally Lunn, an eighteenth century English baker, who perfected a hot, flat, rounded cake, made from sweet yeast dough. Sally had a totally ungovernable temper, and could hit a customer at twenty paces.

(b) Named after Sally Viking O'Hare (1768–1861), the most boring conversationalist in the entire history of Dublin society. Miss O'Hare once ensnared the bishop of Galway on a chaise-longue for three and a half hours on the subject of nail clippings, until His Grace threw a bowl of crab apples at her.

(c) Named after Aunt Sally, a well-known character around the Ridings, or travelling shows of the late eighteenth century, in the Midlands. She had no real skills, except the ability to dodge missiles. Aunt Sally was never to be seen without a filthy old clay pipe stuck between her gums, as she cackled challenges at her public, offering her own head as a target.

CASANOVA
male lover of many women

(a) Named after Algernon Hubert Casanova (1891–1918), who is reputed to have made love to the Tzarina of all the Russias and her four daughters at Christmas dinner, between the soup and the fish course.

(b) Named after Luigi 'Wall-nuts' Casanova (1831–1938), the father of forty-eight children. Casanova modelled for Whistler's noted painting 'Custer's last Stand'.

(c) Named after Giovanni Jacapo Casanova de Seingalt (1725–98). Singer, soldier, magician, spy, preacher, abbé, alchemist, thief, gambler, prisoner, violinist, poet, librarian, autobiographer and lover.

CHAUVINIST
ultra nationalist

(a) Named after George Bernard Shaw (1845–1939), playwright, journalist, critic, inventor of alphabets and possessed of a deep loathing for anything emanating from outside Dublin.

(b) Named after Nicolas Chauvin (?–1815), a French laughing stock who was so devoted to Napoleon that he lost several parts of his anatomy fighting for his emperor. Napoleon rewarded him with a red ribbon.

(c) Named after Mel Chauvinist-Pigge (1925–79), despicable American male supremacist and night clubber. His character was used in the entertainment 'Nine til Five'.

DOUBTING THOMAS
a sceptic

(a) Named after Thomas Doughty, harpooner to Captain Ahab in Herman Melville's novel *Moby Dick*. Thomas did not believe in the existence of the great white whale, until it broke his back.

(b) Named after Thomas the Aspostle. Legend has it that only the sight of the marks of the nails in the hands and feet, and of the spear in the torso would convince the saint that his Christ was alive.

(c) Named after Thomas Tooson (1911–   ), founder of the Flat Earth Society, the Pia Zadora fan club and secretary to the Geneva peace talks.

EPICUREAN
seeking physical gratification

(a) Named after Brian 'Epi' Epstein (1928–67), mentor and manager of the Beatles. Epstein committed suicide after a meteoric career dogged by sex and drugs and rock'n'roll.

(b) Named after Epicurus (340–270 BC), Athenian philosopher, moralist and teacher of ethics, logic and physics. His pupils, slaves, men and women lived together in a communist, virtuous group.

(c) Named after Epicurian (AD 270–340), organizer and promoter of gladiatorial combats, Christian-eating events and sponsored orgies.

JEZEBEL
unfaithful, scheming woman

(a) Named after Jeza Bell (1813–31), a headstrong orthodontist from Croydon, who was unfaithful to her husband with a priest and a small choir during their wedding ceremony in 1821.

(b) Named after Jess Abel (?–1891), gay American gunslinger, who often rode into the sunset mounting a white horse.

(c) Named after Jezebel, the wife of Ahab (*First Book of Kings, ch 19–21*). She shared the throne with her husband, but her lies and wicked affairs angered the people. Jezebel was thrown from a high window and trampled to death by horse-drawn chariots.

LUNATIC
crazy person

(a) Named after Lunaticus (268–200 BC), Roman mystic and hermit, who spent the last thirty years of his life inside a large clay jar.

(b) Named after Luna, Roman goddess of the moon and ancient calendar girl. Her followers and their dogs tended towards over-excitement during the full moon.

(c) Named after Father Terence Looney (1949–   ), priest at The Holy Virgin Mother Church, Dollis Hill, who sends the Reverend Ian Paisley Christmas cards.

LUSH
drunkard, but not from beer

(a) Named after Alderman Lushington, a London brewer and local worthy, who emigrated to Australia and offended a drunken, boorish continent with his drunkeness and boorishness.

(b) Named after Lucy Lush (1881–1940), a popular singer who made several recordings for Imperial Records in the 1920s, before drinking herself into oblivion.

(c) Named after Eduardo 'Luscious' Lucio (1881–1940), cocktails barman at the Café Royale, inventor of the Harvey Wallbanger, and dispenser of the Brewers' Droop.

MATA HARI
seductive female spy

(a) Named after Mata Hari (1889–1924). Eurasian goddess of the silent screen, who caused shocked criticism for her portrayals in *Birth of a Nation*, *The Seven Deadly Sins*, and *Emanuelle goes wee wee*.

(b) Named after Lady Margaretha Geertruida Macleod, alias, Margaretha Zelle, alias Mata Hari (1876–1917), Dutch courtesan, dancer, colonial officer's wife, spy. Shot by the French for allegedly spying for the Germans.

(c) Named after Mother Hurry, the unscrupulously scheming but irresistible spy in Oscar Wilde's *No sex please we're hypocrites*.

MARTINET
severe disciplinarian

(a) Named after Corporal Martinet Himmelheimer, the sadistic ex-postman depicted in *All Quiet on the Western Front* by Erich Maria Remarque. Martinet repeatedly ordered his men to crawl through mud.

(b) Named after General Lawrence Martinet (1864–1928), who forced his regiment to listen to Gilbert and Sullivan operettas for one hour before breakfast.

(c) Named after M Martinet, a late seventeenth century French officer, who served under Louis XIV. He became detested for inventing hundreds of repetitive and tedious drills for foot soldiers.

MOONIE
benign or insidious twit

(a) Named after Keith Moon (1942–75), outrageous drummer with The Who, wrecker of hotel rooms, drum kits and his personal health.

(b) Named after the 'Reverend' Sun Myung Moon in 1954, South Korean billionaire, film director and sect leader, whose followers in the Unification Church undergo a process of brainwashing.

(c) Named after Moonbeam, a simple-minded fairy in *A Midsummer Night's Dream*, by William Shakespeare.

QUISLING
traitor, betrayer of one's own, for base motives

(a) Named after Quisling, a silver-tongued Flemish minstrel at the court of Richard the Lionheart, who sold his mother to a Scottish pedlar in exchange for a digital watch.

(b) Named after Vidkun Quisling (1887–1945), Norwegian Minister of Defence and founder of the Fascist Party in 1933, he prepared his country for invasion by Germany and became the Nazis' puppet President. He was shot for his crimes.

(c) Named after Qawi Zling (1948–   ), wife of an Iranian diplomat to Britain, and allowed to live in the United Kingdom by the generosity of the Home Office, who has to date shoplifted over two million pounds worth of polyester-cotton lingerie from British Home Stores.

SCROOGE
miser, cantankerous meany

(a) Named after Howard Scrooge (1911–77), American multi-millionaire aviator, film magnate, newspaper owner and deranged recluse.

(b) Named after Ebeneezer Scrooge (1843), the central character of Dickens' magnificent *A Christmas Carol*. Anyone who maintains that Christmas is humbug cannot be all bad.

(c) Named after SCROOGE, the Swiss Central Organisation of Grant Exemptions, despicable organ of the Zurich bankers who refuse to lend third world nations the odd billion.

SILLY BILLY
foolish person, blockhead

(a) Named after William the Conqueror (1027–84), who set off for Le Havre to visit his friends the Cohens and landed in Hastings by mistake.

(b) Named after William Frederick, who became Duke of Gloucester in 1805. The derogatory nickname was coined by himself to describe himself, during a heated wrangle between Whigs and Tories.

(c) Named after William Pitt the Younger (1759–1806), who thought that he could solve the problems of Ireland.

TROLLOP
ignorant and ill-bred woman, often associated with loose morals

(a) Named after Mimsy Trollop, a minor character in *The Old Curiosity Shop* by Charles Dickens. She is depicted as a sluttish gin-sodden young woman, who proves to have a heart of gold.

(b) Named after Frances Trollope (1780–1863), mother of Anthony. She was ridiculed for her Englishness whilst visiting America, and on her return she published *Domestic Manners of the Americans* in 1832. The book offended most of American society.

(c) Named after Trallopia, the wife of Quintus Fabius Ambustus, Roman conqueror of Gaul. She was slovenly and vulgar, and not tolerated by Roman society.

XENOPHOBIC
fear of foreigners

(a) Named after Dan Xeno (1845–1911), British music hall comic who refused all offers of work outside England.

(b) Named after General Xenophon (431–355 BC), disciple of Socrates, who led an army of 10,000 warriors to the Black Sea to protect his tribe.

(c) Named after Z Q Xenoph (1939–   ). Conceived during a game of scrabble, Mr Xenoph has problems at immigration.

13 THINGS TO STICK IN YOUR MOUTH

BIRDSEYE
frozen food

(a) Named after Captain Clarence Birdseye in 1924, who transported deep frozen vegetables across the high seas, me hearties.

(b) Named after Estelle Bird in 1952. Originally custard manufacturer's, the new convenience foods were first marketed under the slogan 'Birds Aye!'

(c) Named after Jimmy 'Birdseye' Guano in 1892. Guano performed in revolting freak shows, sucking eyes out of dead bird's heads. His autopsy revealed a stomach full of small glass beads.

BLOODY MARY
vodka and tomato juice

(a) Named after Mary Kinney-Baker (1879–1960), owner of the famed Ma Baker's Club in New York. She invented the drink during prohibition, to mask the taste of alcohol.

(b) Named after Mary Tudor (1516–58), daughter of Henry VIII and Catherine of Aragon. Mary re-established Roman Catholicism in Britain during her short reign, by ordering hundreds of Protestants to be beheaded.

(c) Named after Mary Pickford (1893–1983), Canadian silent-screen goddess and Hollywood's richest star of the day. Mary is reputed to have been blind drunk for the filming of most of her greatest scenes.

GRANNY SMITH
green, crisp apple, better than those French imports

(a) Named after Maria Ann Smith, Australian horticulturist, who first bred the apple in New South Wales at the turn of the century.

(b) Named after Granny Smith (?–1713), the Green Witch of Wookey Hole. The old lady was condemned to trial by water for alleged witchcraft in the waters of the underground lake at Wookey. A single green apple bobbed to the surface to mark her strange disappearance.

(c) Named after Maureen Clyfanwyr Smith (1860–1931), President of the Women's Royal Voluntary Society. Green with envy, rotten to the core, she gave David Lloyd George the pip.

GREENGAGE
small fruit

(a) Named after Jock 'Bender' Greengage (1897–1936), a small, hairy fruit.

(b) Named after Phileda Green (1643–1707). This unfortunate lady suffered a unique deformity, being cursed with a nose that closely resembled the unripened berry. Her proboscis is preserved in Bulgaria where it is an object of some veneration.

(c) Named after Sir William Gage of Suffolk in 1725, by none other than Sir William Gage, who usurped the label from its previous donor, the queen of Francis I of France.

GROG
booze, particularly rum

GROGGY
to feel under the weather, suffering a hang-over

(a) Named after the Norse god Groga, the Scandinavian equivalent to Bacchus. During the mid-winter festival, hot, spiced ale is drunk to excess. The word was introduced to the English language as long ago as 200 BC.

(b) Named after Kenneth Anthony Grogan, Victualler to the Portsmouth Dockyard around 1772–5, who was justifiably accused of watering down and adulterating barrels of rum. He was hung in a cage from the Sally-port for one week, to pay for his sins.

(c) Named after Admiral 'Old Grog' Edward Vernon (1684–1757), who was wont to wear a grogram cloak in rotten weather. Popular with the fleet for introducing the rum ration in 1740, he was dismissed six years later for writing seditious pamphlets against the admiralty.

LOGANBERRY
dark red, fleshy berry

(a) Named after Jimmy Logan (1921–), Scottish comedian and actor, who starred in a children's television series called 'Loganberry Pie'. Logan did much to popularize the berry, which was formally known as the Crudworzel.

(b) Named after Joshua Loganber (1777–1842), first President of the Royal Horticultural Society, who became obsessed with the quest for a 'universal fruit'. He is buried under the pagoda in Kew Gardens.

(c) Named after James H Logan (1841–1928), American lawyer, ox driver, teacher, telegraph pole pioneer and Superior Court Judge. He crossed a blackberry with a raspberry in 1881.

MELBA
cold dessert, usually of ice cream and peaches

(a) Named after Helen Mitchel (1861–1931), who changed her name to Melba because she was passionately in love with Melbourne, Australia, the city in which she was conceived.

(b) Named after Giacomo 'Pretty Boy' Melba, (1872–1928), Chicago gangster and part-time ice cream waiter, who instigated the horrific Ice Cream War, as a result of an insult regarding a bruised peach.

(c) Named after Dame Nelly Melba (1847–1919), the first Australian superstar, and coiner of the phrase; 'Isn't this peachy.' She was addicted to this dish, and died vastly overweight when her heart gave out during a tour of the Empire.

MICKEY FINN
a drugged drink

(a) Named after Mikhael 'The Finn' Rjamoku (1803–72), bareknuckle heavyweight boxer, who inexplicably lost his championship by falling asleep during the match, after drinking a glass of milk.

(b) Named after Michael, Dauphin of the Holy Roman Empire (1431–85), suspected of having murdered Pope Leo XI with a cup of poisoned wine.

(c) Named after Mickey Finn (1846–1906), a Chicago bartender whose hobby was to doctor his customers' drinks with chloral hydrate, and rob them after they passed out.

NICOTINE
addictive substance, contained in tobacco and heavily taxed

(a) Named after Nico Tine (1899–1940), Italian American Ice Cream King, whose 'adult' flavours included Old Shag, Readyrubbed and Ashe. Many of his friends died of lung disease.

(b) Named after Dr Anselm Nicotine (1738–1802), a Dutchman, who used concentrated extract of tobacco mixed with oil as a palliative for practically every ailment suffered by his patients.

(c) Named after Jean Nicot, Lord of Villemain, French Ambassador to Portugal. In 1561 Nicot brought a gift of smoking tobacco to the Grand Prior of France. Its fame and popularity spread quickly, and never encountered the royal opposition experienced in England.

PAVLOVA
meringue filled with tropical fruit and covered in cream

(a) Named after Percy Pavlova (1902–71), pastry cook to Her Gracious Majesty Queen Salote of Tonga, and later Liberace.

(b) Named after Pa Vulva, the lovable glutton featured in R Soles' whimsical cartoon strip 'Meet the Cleavers'.

(c) Named after Anna Pavlova (1881–1931), daughter of a laundress and creator of the 'dying swan.' The dish was invented to mark her ballet dancing in Australia.

PETER STUYVESANT
branded cigarette

(a) Named after Peter Stuyvesant (1892–1972). A Rhodesian cigarette manufacturer, who set up the first assembly line to mass produce packets of twenty cigarettes, cutting his prices by thirty per cent over his hand-rolled competitors.

(b) Named after Peter Stuyvesant (1792–1872). A Dutch tobacco grower who owned vast estates in Virginia, USA which were worked by slaves. He is reputed to have invented the cigarette, before which time all tobacco was smoked in cigar form, in pipes, or was chewed.

(c) Named after Peter Stuyvesant (1592–1672), the Dutch governor of New Amsterdam, who surrendered to the British in 1664, after which the city was named New York. He retired to his farm, the Bouwerij, which gave its name to the Bowery district.

SANDWICH
slices of bread, sometimes buttered, interleaved with sundry foods

(a) Named after Lord Aristotle Sandwich (1718–92), Maitre des Cinque Ports. Sandwich ordered his clerks to eat these grim objects whilst working at their desks, thereby saving conventional meal-times.

(b) Named after Berthold Wurstlieber Sonderwitsch (1804–71), the giant Hussar and noted glutton, who choked to death in a Dresden delicatessen attempting to swallow a cream of herring, strawberry and liver gateau, muttering 'no salt . . .'

(c) Named after John Jemmy Twitcher Montagu, Fourth Earl of Sandwich (1718–92). First Lord of the Admiralty, member of the Hell-Fire Club, blackguard, and corruptor of the navy, he invented sandwiches to sustain his vile body while gambling till dawn with the other cads.

TOM COLLINS
a cocktail based on gin

(a) Named after Tom Collins, the bartender who worked at Limmers Old House in nineteenth century London. Collins did his best to disguise the foul nature of impure gin. His most famous invention is the Singapore Sling.

(b) Named after Tom Collins (1872–1926), an Irish farmer who emigrated to Chicago in 1889, and founder of his own distillery at the age of twenty. Collins was murdered by mobsters and his body delivered to his family in thirteen parcels.

(c) Named after Thomas Cullin (1794–1871). A Bristol born poet and drunk, Cullin's characters included Theresa Green, Duane Pipe, Orson Cart, Mary Christmas and Tamara Knight.

ALBERT
a watch-chain worn across a waistcoat

(a) Named after Albert Ross (?–1895), an ancient mariner who secured his chronometer thus to prevent it dropping over the side.

(b) Named after Prince Albert (1819–61), husband of Queen Victoria. In 1849 the jewellers of Birmingham presented him with such a chain, and he wore it until his death.

(c) Named after Albert, a mechanical man constructed for the Great Exhibition of 1849. Albert was supposed to do a clockwork dance, but was thwarted by a ruptured chain link.

BELCHER
blue scarf with white spots

(a) Named after Sir Toby Belch in Shakespeare's *Twelfth Night*:

> 'Come Sir, thine kerchief doth lend somber aspect to such reuben jowl, of white on blue no politik we make . . .'

(b) Named after Stoner Baines Belcher (1893–1931). Playboy Ambassador of the USA to Turkey, Belcher was found strangled with a woman's scarf, and a list of his many indiscretions fastened to his wrist with a skewer.

(c) Named after Jem Belcher (1781–1811), a popular pugilist, butcher and one-eyed publican. Belcher was defeated by Tom Gibb in 1809, and retired from the ring.

He was renowned for sporting the blue and white scarf wherever he went.

BLOOMERS
lengthy knickers, faux pas

(a) Named after Deitrich Arlene Bloomer (1803–51), Dutch silk importer and conceited dancer, who in 1851 produced this undergarment in two sizes, large and very large.

(b) Named after Horace Walpole Bloomer (1803–51), vicar of All Saints, Dunstable. In 1849, being of unsound mind, he addressed his congregation on the subject of 'Am I my brother's keeper?' minus his trousers.

(c) Named after Mrs Amelia Jencks Bloomer, who inaugurated this item of clothing on a solemn occasion in 1851. The bold New York lady sported a skirt to just below her knees, under which she wore pantaloons tied at the ankles, all for the sake of her new-found hobby, bicycling.

BLUCHERS
leather half-boots

(a) Named after Field Marshal Gerhard L Von Blucher, the Prussian army commander at the battle of Waterloo, whose victory column overlooks the Brandenburg Gate, in Berlin.

(b) Named after Otto Blucher (1794–1849), a Potsdam shoemaker. Blucher invented the jackboot just in case anyone invented the Nazis.

(c) Named after Arthur Wellesley, First Duke of Wellington (1769–1852), whose boot was first referred to in 1817. The Iron Duke died at the age of eighty-three in his armchair with his boots on.

CARDIGAN
knitted woollen jacket

(a) Named after James Thomas Budenell, seventh Earl of Cardigan (1797–1868), the leader of the ill-fated Six Hundred at the Battle of Balaclava, where the matching woolly helmet was fashionable. He was tried for the crime of duelling in 1841 by the House of Lords.

(b) Named after Herbert Rudolph Cardigan (1806–83), a carpet manufacturer, who invented the knitting machine and two-ply wool.

(c) Named after Larry Cardigan (1973–), the Welsh mystic who believed that woollens were the key to the universe. Happily married to a sheep, he lived soberly near Cardiff Arms Park, subsisting on a diet of grass and raising his family.

COTY
packaged paint and smells

(a) Named after Cosi Fan Coty (1803–89), Parisian perfumer and entrepreneur who invented the bulb spray dispenser. The Maison Coty began selling mouthwash in 1872.

(b) Named after Mouchette Helene Coty (1892–1961). Coty was instrumental in the wholesale slaughter of the magnificent sperm whale, to satiate the hairs of the French female armpit.

(c) Named after François Joseph Sportuno Coty (1874–1934). An extreme nationalist and splendid Corsican journalist who owned *Le Figaro*. Coty gained a fortune and then lost it. He was finally sued by his wife, who divorced him, and died a broken ruined genius.

GEORGETTE
finely textured, thin silk crepe

(a) Named after Georgette Heyer, writer of thin textured, fine silk crepe.

(b) Named after Madame Georgette de la Plante, the French modiste. She was influential in the late nineteenth and early twentieth centuries, and popularized this fabric.

(c) Named after Cecilia B de Mille (1870–1900), alias Georgette, dancer at the Folies Bergère. Georgette used layers of this gossamer to perform her famous 'Dance of the Seven Veils'.

JAEGERS
woollen clothing

(a) Named after Dr Gustav Jaeger, who in 1890 first marketed in England his night apparel, slippers and underclothes, manufactured by Doctor Jaeger's Sanitary Woollen System Company Limited.

(b) Named after Lady Christal Jaegers (1871–1934). London socialite and advocate of women's rights, she popularized this type of clothing on the hunting, fishing and shooting circuit.

(c) Named after Henry Sean Jaeger (1812–86), whose

hosiery establishment was opened in the Burlington Arcade in 1867.

KNICKERS
undergarment worn below the belt and above the knee

(a) Named after Monica Knickers (1882–1940), surly campaigner for women's rights, who removed her underwear at Royal Ascot in 1911 and frightened the King's horses.

(b) Named after Louis B Knicker (1816–79), Lancashire clothier, who designed and promoted bicycling apparel for both ladies and gentlemen.

(c) Named after Diedrich Knickerbocker, the professed writer of Washington Irving's *History of New York* (1809), whose illustrations showed men wearing such garments. The Knickerbocker family arrived in America from Holland in 1670.

LEOTARD
one piece gymnastic or dancing suit

(a) Named after Leo Tard (1317–89), the minstrel who wandered across Europe searching for his lost daughter, singing strange ballads. He always dressed in a single black garment, vowing to wear bright colours only when his quest was fulfilled.

(b) Named after Jules Leotard (1842–90), celebrated French acrobat who performed the first aerial somersault. He invented the tight-fitting garment to highlight his private parts for his female audience.

(c) Named after Pope Leo VII (1411–58), who disregarded traditional papal garb in favour of simple clothing. 'Leo le tard' referred to his inability to arrive on time for any occasion.

MACINTOSH
waterproof overcoat

(a) Named after Igor Lillette Macintosh (1830–71), the deformed keeper of the Wax Museum of the Rue Morgue, Bognor Regis, who engaged in the vile series of rubber-dippings for his ironically named Living Tableaux.

(b) Named after Charles Macintosh (1766–1843). A Scottish chemist, he distilled coal-tar to produce naptha for the impregnation of cloth, and sandwiched a layer of rubber between two layers of this material. He produced his topcoat in 1823, and by 1836 all waterproof coats were called after him.

(c) Named after Sir Harold Macintosh, (1884–1962), British Ambassador to the United Arab Enemas, Sir Harold devoted most of his spare time to rubber wear.

MAE WEST
inflatable lifejacket, particularly for airmen; cockney rhyming slang for 'a breast'

(a) Named after Mae West (1892–1983), wicked lady of the 1930s silver screen and geriatric vamp, who coined outrageous clichés including: 'Is that a pistol in yer pocket or are ya just pleased ta see me?' The lifejacket was said to resemble her bust line.

(b) Named after Anna Mae West (1916–71), Euro-Chinese star of the wartime drama 'Chocks Away!' in which the heroine smuggles a V2 rocket out of Nazi Germany in her brassière.

(c) Named after J D Mae-West (1882–1956), parachute manufacturer and pedigree toad breeder, with an undeserved reputation for shoddy goods, although a few of his toads were a little highly strung.

RAGLAN
sleeve and overcoat

(a) Named after Field Marshal Fitzroy Somerset, First Baron Raglan (1788–1855). The victor at the Battle of Inkerman, Raglan lost an arm at Waterloo, and rode on a padded saddle designed for a one-legged rider.

(b) Named after Monty Raglan (1860–1927), rotund Nottingham sweat-shop proprietor. Raglan produced gentlemen's clothing of the highest quality for the lowest wages.

(c) Named after Mrs Dorothy Raglan (1904–71), foremost society outfitter and confidante of many crowned heads. She revealed more than the odd gussett in her sensational book of memoirs, *Which side do you hang?* published in 1968.

SAM BROWNE
brown military belt supported by a shoulder strap

(a) Named after General Sir Samuel Browne VC (1824–1901), one-armed hero of the Indian Mutiny.

(b) Named after Sam Browne, the hero of Stanley Hollo-way's comic monologue, 'Sam, pick up thy musket', first recorded in 1928.

(c) Named after Samantha Browne (1900–67), the original 'gay young thing' who shocked society by exposing one breast at Ascot in 1924.

WELLINGTON BOOT
calf-length waterproof footwear

(a) Named after Wellington F A Boot (1961–). Mr Boot has twice been apprehended by the Norfolk Con-stabulary in the act of paedophilia, that is to say, having carnal knowledge of footwear.

(b) Named after John Churchill, First Duke of Wellington (1438–1506). Nicknamed 'Old Ironsides', Wellington redesigned the fighting armour of his infantry, greatly reducing its weight and increasing his soldiers' effectiveness. The boot was waterproofed with tar impregnated hemp.

(c) Named after Arthur Wellesley, First Duke of Welling-ton (1769–1852), whose boot was first referred to in 1817. The Iron Duke died aged eighty-three, in his armchair, with his boots on.

9 THINGS TO PUT ON YOUR HEAD

BOWLER

black hat, as worn by Bolivian peasant women, English gentlemen and members of the Orange Order

(a) Named after Thomas and William Bowler in 1849.

Mr Coke: Sirs, I am constantly being beaten about the head by overhanging foliage whilst engaged in shooting small creatures.

Bowler: Sir, this protective headgear, being second to none, will pass any test you might care to make.

Coke: I will hereby test the strength by standing upon it ... and perceiving no indentation, beg your permission to jump upon its crown.

Bowler: That will be twelve shillings, Sir.

Coke: Splendid! Henceforth this hat will be known as Coke!

(b) Named after Georges Beaulieu in 1809.

Coke: Explain, Monsieur, the relevance of sunhats for our female labourers.

Beaulieu: Sir, the headgear before you offers shading from the sun, protection against the tree snake, and a useful eating vessel.

Coke: I will take one hundred of your hats. What are they called?

Beaulieu: Naturally Sir, I call this hat a Beaulieu!

(c) Named after Herbert Bowler in 1892.

Coke: Gentlemen, we have commissioned Mr Bowler to make this helmet for us, which to the untrained eye appears to be quite innocent.

Bowler: Protection for the Loyalist head.

Coke: Splendid! Henceforth this hat will be known as a Bowler.

BUSBY

tall furry head-dress of a Hussar, orginally of bearskin, now of nylon

(a) Named after Richard Busby (1606–95), an unpopular pedagogue and harsh disciplinarian. Busby affected an enormous wig, but was too fearsome to be laughed at.

(b) Named after General Richard Busby (1706–95), who redesigned the uniform of the Hussars, and was killed at the age of eighty-nine while out horse riding.

(c) Named after Richard Busby (1806–95), hatmaker and eccentric. His original design for the commissioned head-dress was over four feet tall, and weighed twenty-four pounds.

POE

portable private convenience

(a) Named after Silas Poe, the well meaning friend of Sam Weller in Dickens' *Pickwick Papers*. Poe was unable to finish any conversation without having to slip outside to relieve himself.

(b) Named after Po, the Cheyenne god of buffalo excrement.

(c) Named after Edgar Allan Poe (1809–49), horror story writer, whose poems and stories led to involuntary evacuation. Orphaned at two, a disaster in university, the US army and love, he turned to drink, drugs and the macabre.

POMPADOUR
affected hair style, dressed high and brushed back, beloved of teddy boys and royalty

(a) Named after Pompah Dour, the supremely miserable Chief Wardle and Barber-Royale in the Gilbert and Sullivan operetta, *The Eager Herring*.

(b) Named after Jeanne Antoinette Poison Le-Normant d'Etoiles (1721–64), who pupated into the bewigged Madame de Pompadour after becoming Louis XV's mistress, and dominating his weak will.

(c) Named after The Pompadums (1954), Bengali rock 'n' roll band who had a brief taste of stardom in the US with their disc, 'It's my chapathi'. Fans copied their ghee-oiled hair-do's, and the vogue lingers still.

SIDEBURNS
earward facial hair

(a) Named after Ambrose Everett Burnside (1824–81), Union general, catastrophically beaten by Confederate General Robert E Lee. Burnside survived to become a US senator, where his whiskers were celebrated.

(b) Named after George Burns (1884–), laconic American comedian, who sported an exaggerated hairstyle in his career, but clean shaved as soon as he gained success.

(c) Named after Rupert Brynsly Swynburne (1771–1850), atrocious poet and sheep stealer. When he went bald at the age of thirty, Rupert combed his side whiskers across the top of his foul head.

STETSON
an article of headgear, favoured by Hollywood cowboys

(a) Named after Arnold Praisegod Stetson (1808–70), who inherited a successful hatters business employing 200 workers producing 100,000 hats a year. Stetson was a complete fool, and foundered in 1856, bankrupt.

(b) Named after John Batterson Stetson (1830–1906), who developed his one man hat business into a plant of 3,500 workers producing 2,000,000 hats a year. Stetson was a great benefactor, and founded the University at DeLand Florida.

(c) Named after Jesse 'Slowhand' Stetson (1841–1910), gunfighter, horse-molester and drunk, who was never known to remove his hat during the last forty years of his miserable life.

TAM O'SHANTER
a woolly hat with a pompom

(a) Named after Tam Dalyell (1925–   ) firebrand Labour MP and scourge of the Thatcher Government. Mr Dalyell popularized this headgear by sporting a red woolly hat during the budget address of 1972.

(b) Named after Tam O'Shanter, the hero of Robert Burns' poem written in 1789. Tam was based on a local farmer, Douglas Graham.

(c) Named after Tom The Chanter (1321–80). A Franciscan monk who formalized the written notation of plainsong at the monastery of Wimbourne Abbas. After a scandalous liaison with a local lady, he fled to Scotland and became a hermit.

TRILBY
black, soft felt hat

(a) Named after the novel of that title, written by George du Maurier in 1894. Beerbohm Tree wore such a hat in the stage play when he played Svengali, the sinister influence on Trilby, a young artist's model.

(b) Named after Trilby, alias Josephine Sachs (1903–58), the actress and fashion model. She favoured masculine clothing in stark black and white, and achieved her greatest notoriety in 1931 when she appeared in 'Hot nuts over London', wearing a black floppy hat and a bow tie.

(c) Named after Messrs Trilby and Trilby, hat-makers of Dublin, who first produced these hats in 1902 for Oscar Wilde.

TUREEN
a large bowl

(a) Named after Visconte de Twenne (1611–75), Marshal General of France, who supped soup from his military helmet.

(b) Named after Brydie Tween (1835–96), a celebrated Belfast cook, who specialized in highly spiced stews which she prepared in a large double-handle bowl.

(c) Named after Matthew de la Ture (1777–1848), inventor of a small device for urination while attending speeches in the Houses of Parliament.

USEFULL WEDDING PRESENTS

BLANKET
slumber cover

(a) Named after Thomas Blanket in 1340. A British
weaver, Thomas invented this convenience before
which straw or fur had been used.

(b) Named after Blanquette, the twelfth century French
hermit, who walked from Lyon to Constantinople clad
in sacking.

(c) Named after Blangeld, Norse god of sleep and bedwet-
ting.

CHESTERFIELD
a stuffed and buttoned sofa

(a) Named after Chester Field, the limping deputy to Matt
Dillon in the television series 'Gunsmoke'. When his leg
played up, Chester would recline on such a sofa, and
rub his limb with horse linament.

(b) Named after Hedley Rudyard Chesterfield (1792–
1884), cabinet-maker and upholsterer, who designed
the seating in both the Houses of Lords and Commons.

(c) Named after Philip Dorner Stanhope (1694–1773)
Fourth Earl of Chesterfield, Ambassador to the Hague,
Viceroy of Ireland and writer of 400 letters to his bas-
tard son, concerning sex, power and ambition. He
needed the sofa for rest.

CHIPPENDALE
stylized furniture

(a) Named after Josiah Chippendale (1802–73), carpenter and lay preacher. Chippendale was cathedral organist at Leicester for the last twenty years of his life. He invented the fret saw, and introduced 'japanned' lacquer to Britain.

(b) Named after Chip'n'Dale, those saucy, lovable chipmonks, brought to us by the late, great Walt Disney. Their wood-nibbling, rib-tickling escapades in furniture alteration have won them a place in the world's waste disposal units.

(c) Named after Thomas Chippendale (1718–79), who married the styles of Louis XV, the Rococo, and the Gothic with a little Chinese thrown for good measure. He introduced the claw and ball foot to the world, and launched cabriole legs. In 1754 Chippendale published *The Gentleman and Cabinet-Maker's Dictionary*.

DAVENPORT
narrow, folding writing desk, also a large sofa-bed

(a) Named after Nigel Davenport (1928–   ), roguish British actor, who won great acclaim for his portrayals of well-made furniture.

(b) Named after Captain Davenport in 1820, an English sailor, who commissioned a Lancashire carpenter to build furniture for his cabin, from his original designs.

(c) Named after Josiah Davenport (1733–1812), a dwarf who espoused a large lady. He designed all his family furniture, including an adjustable commode.

DEMIJOHN
over-large bulging bottle, with a very narrow neck

(a) Named after Dame Jeanne, an over-large bulging French lady, with a very narrow neck.

(b) Named after Dr P P Demijohn (1760–1812), the inventor of the bedpan.

(c) Named after Dimitri Johanes (1698–1758), a famed entertainer who played musical water-filled bottles, and composed the tune of the child's rhyme 'Ten Green Bottles'.

DOILY
lace mat, placed on a polished surface to impress guests

(a) Named after Dolly Grey, the early nineteenth century singer and dancer, who performed in a loosely cro-chéted leotard (*qv*) which gave tantalizing views of her body, and boosted the London sales of the newly invented opera-glass.

(b) Named after Madame D'Oillex (1674–1739), who affected a preposterous tall wig, made from human hair and lace. She was rumoured to have been the cause of the despicable Guerre des Glaces.

(c) Named after Messrs Doily, of the Strand, London, famous seventeenth century drapers, and purveyors of very hairy cloth.

JEROBOAM
very large bottle, often associated with champagne

(a) Named after Jeroboam, First King of Israel, as featured in the *Book of Kings*, ch XIII, vs 22.

(b) Named after Sir Joshua Jeroboam (1731–1807), a widower by profession, who had his beloved wife pickled in a very large bottle.

(c) Named after Jerry Boam (?–1568), a London brewer, who was the first man in England to produce bottled beer.

SHERATON
'Directoire' style furniture

(a) Named after Thomas Sheraton (1751–1806), born in Stockton-on-Tees, died in Soho, a pauper. Sheraton wrote many religious works as well as designing innovative furniture, the designs of which were usually stolen and copied.

(b) Named after Lord Alexander Sheraton (1820–87), first Lord of the Colonial Office, who shipped vast quantities of furniture to the many British embassies, missions and governors' offices around the world.

(c) Named after Victor Sherat (1793–1887), Parisian designer and entrepreneur. His factory produced wall coverings, fabrics and glassware as well as furnishings.

SPODE
a type of porcelain

(a) Named after Ebenezer Spode (1806–79), doll-maker to the royal children of Europe. His exquisite collection of hand-painted heads, hands and eyes may be viewed at the Victoria and Albert museum.

(b) Named after Josiah Spode (1754–1827) of Stoke-on-Trent. Spode stole the willow pattern from the

Japanese, and made his plates from crunched up bones, rocks and paste.

(c) Named after S Pode (1864–1959) of Scunthorpe. Pode specialized in commodes for war veterans, and once met George Formby in an elevator.

TEDDY BEAR
furry bear doll

(a) Named after Teddy (?–1885), a giant black bear of the London Zoo. Sold to Barnum's Circus in 1882, Teddy was killed by a railway engine three years later.

(b) Named after Edward Bear, the godfather of Winnie the Pooh, in A A Milne's children's book, *The House at Pooh Corner*.

(c) Named after Theodore Roosevelt (1859–1919), President of the United States from 1901–07 and a notorious hunter of bears. He donated several cubs to the Bronx Zoo, and the phrase 'teddy bear' was coined in 1906.

WEDGWOOD
stylized pottery

(a) Named after Josiah Clement Wedgwood (1730–95). Losing one leg because of the pox, he became Queen's Potter in 1762. Wedgwood opened his Etruria works in 1769, after his interest in Etruscan vases.

(b) Named after Thomas Greville Wedgwood (1778–1841). Famed for his designs in relief, Wedgwood lost both of his front teeth trying to crack a walnut, during the Christmas of 1812.

(c) Named after Thomas Josiah Wedgwood (1696–1768). Son of Josiah, the famous Stockton-on-Trent porcelain manufacturer, Thomas used sulphates to pigment his subtly coloured pottery. He lost a thumb after his dog, Satan, attacked him in bed.

PUBLIC
CONVENIENCES

ANDERSON SHELTER
domestic air raid protection

(a) Named after Sir John Anderson in 1939. Anderson was Home Secretary for two years at the beginning of the Second World War, at which time this air raid shelter was installed in thousands of British back gardens.

(b) Named after Moira Anderson, by the Royal Society for the Prevention of Cruelty to Animals in 1973, and intended for household pets to hide inside during 'Stars on Sunday'.

(c) Named after Hans Christian Anderson in 1856. Such a shelter was described in detail in his charming fairy story *The Tin Soldier*.

BELISHA BEACON
flashing yellow globe atop a pole, indicating a pedestrian crossing

(a) Named after Maldor Belisha (?–1239), outlaw hero who was active in Essex. He was never caught, being helped by sympathetic villagers who would light beacons to warn him of approaching danger.

(b) Named after Otto Szczelkun, alias Belisha (1861–1940). Belisha was one of the world's most loved clowns. He travelled Europe for over sixty years, delighting audiences in his skinny body-stocking of black and white stripes, and his big yellow false nose.

(c) Named after Leslie Hore-Belisha (1893–1940), who was Minister of Transport from 1934 to 1937. A former president of the Oxford Union, Belisha introduced many safety measures aimed at cutting down road accidents.

BIG BEN
13½ ton bell which rings out the hour over Westminster

(a) Named after Benjamin Disraeli in 1872, who was Prime Minister at the time, which was a little before noon.

(b) Named after Anthony Wedgwood Benn in 1960. The self-renounced Peer of the Realm was Minister for Industry and Timekeeping in the first Wilson Government.

(c) Named after Sir Benjamin Hall in 1856. Hall was Commissioner of Works when the bell was hung, and the naming followed a long established London tradition.

BURNHAM SCALE
graduation of teachers' salaries

(a) Named after Albert Burnham (1907–51), Minister of Education and Fisheries in the 1948 Labour Cabinet. He was sacked by Clement Attlee in the cabinet reshuffle known as the Night of the Long Hatpins.

(b) Named after Edgar Reece-Horn Burnham (1803–1909), whose solution to unrest in the village schools of Norfolk was to gather together large groups of schoolmistresses and weigh them.

(c) Named after Harry Lawson, First Viscount Burnham, (1862–1935), the Director of the *Daily Telegraph*. Lawson was President of the 1919–20 committee on teacher's pay.

GAMP
stumpy umbrella

(a) Named after Gampini, pupil of Leonardo da Vinci, who constructed the first ever 'modern' umbrella, complete with sprung ribs and walking-stick handle.

(b) Named after Mrs Sairey Gamp, who appeared in *Martin Chuzzlewit* by Charles Dickens. She was a fat old drunken nurse, with a mythical friend named Mr Harris. The umbrella was part of her ritual regalia.

(c) Named after Oliver Gampion (1859–93), the famed Victorian 'Birdman', who plunged to his death from Dover Castle, when his umbrella-like wings collapsed.

HILTON
chain of expensive hotels

(a) Named after Conrad Nicholson Hilton (1887–1980). Born on Christmas day, he rented rooms in a farmhouse for a dollar a day as a boy. Bank clerk, soldier, storekeeper and creator of the largest hotel organization in the world.

(b) Named after Hilton Keynes (1842–1946), insane town planner and author of *The Modern City*. He foresaw vast housing developments based on grid patterns, wherein the population was controlled by television screens.

(c) Named after Adolf Hilton (1887–1945), a talented Austrian interior decorator. He did much to influence hotel accommodation in Europe from 1939 until his untimely death in a Berlin motel.

LISTERINE
antiseptic solution

(a) Named after Emelia Rose Concepta Listerine (1872–1941), hygiene (*qv*) fetishist and founder of the Church of Prevention of the Second Coming.

(b) Named after 'Doctor' Archie K Lister (1806–1890), a travelling quack who was active in the mid-western USA. The doc's medicine was guaranteed to cure your abscess, acidosis, acne, ageing, ague, allergies, anthrax and asthma – and that was only the As.

(c) Named after Joseph, First Baron Lister, of Lyme Regis (1827–1912), a dedicated surgeon, uncommonly preoccupied with sores, suppurations, festerings and pus.

MANSARD
steeply sloping roof, accommodating a garret

(a) Named after Mansard Dormer (1713–81), a German builder, and inventor of the dormer window, the backtrap gulley, and a device for extracting stones out of horses' hooves.

(b) Named after Mansardi (?–1832), a Neapolitan poet and recluse, who shut himself away in his attic for six years while he wrote his epic poem, *Conversations with a stool*.

(c) Named after François Mansard (1598–1666), Parisian architect, and designer of several châteaux. He was an important influence on the appearance of his native city, and much of his work remains today.

MONEY
root of all evil

(a) Named after Munneh, the Hebrew god of Friday nights, goats' bladders and tax evasion.

(b) Named after Juno Moneta, Roman goddess of admonition and advice, in whose temple coins were minted.

(c) Named after Sir Horace Moneyfield (1257–1332), who first introduced the milled edge to coins of the realm to thwart 'clipping'.

RITZ
stylish place

(a) Named after Crawford Ritz (1794–1873), cake and biscuit-maker to Queen Victoria. His crumbly creations were a wonder to behold, a joy to eat, and hell to digest.

(b) Named after 'Ma' Ritziani (?–1893). The awesome land-lady of an East End flophouse. 'The Ritz' passed into cockney folklore, its meaning now conjuring up the complete opposite of its origin.

(c) Named after Cesar Ritz (1815–1918), Swiss-born restaurateur and hotel-keeper extraordinaire. He chose London as the site of his most illustrious premises.

UNION JACK
national flag of the United Kingdom

(a) Named after James Boggeryue (1540–1607), Grand Protector of the Privy Council, and High Herald during the Union of Scotland and England. His design for the unifying flag was said by Roger Bacon to 'resemble a brokene wyndowe . . .'

(b) Named after King James VI of Scotland, who in 1603 was invited to become King James I of England. The amalgamation of flags became known as Jack, after the monarch's signature 'Jacobus'.

(c) Named after Union Jack, the definitive parody of the shop steward, as portrayed by Peter Sellers in the 1961 comedy film *I'm all right Jack*.

WOOLWORTHS
ubiquitous international store

(a) Named after Francis W Woolworth (1882–1949). A native of Bootle, Lancashire, Woolworth invested total capital of £4.10*s*. in reprocessed soap. By the time his friends got worried he was in the shampoo business.

(b) Named after Frank Winfield Woolworth (1852–1919). A native New Yorker, Woolworth invested his total capital of £60 in a cut-price shop in Utica. By the time he died he was worth £9 million.

(c) Named after F W Hutton Woolworth (1891–1960). Opening his first store in 1919 with army-surplus cutlery and socks, he boasted that none of his goods would cost more than ten cents, a pledge he did not break until 1934.

COMMUNICATION CORDS

BOWDLERIZE
prudish expurgation, to delete naughty bits from publications

(a) Named after Elisabeth Bowdler (1911–70), who pioneered the Festival of Light movement, and campaigned against permissiveness and licentiousness on television and in the press.

(b) Named after Thomas Bowdler (1754–1825), who edited the complete works of Shakespeare, leaving out anything that might be considered unsuitable to be read aloud in front of children.

(c) Named after Minge de Baudelaire (1754–1825), who rewrote *Oedipus Rex*, omitting all references to incest.

BRAILLE
system of embossed-relief reading and writing for the blind

(a) Named after Louis Braille (1809–52). Struck blind at three, a professor at the age of seventeen, Braille formulated his praiseworthy system at the Institution des Jeunes Aveugles, Paris.

(b) Named after Pierre Braille (1852–1906), who fell in love with Ariadne Clite, a blind, dumb girl, and spent more than half of his life trying to date her.

(c) Named after Peterjon Braille (1906–52), Dutch Minister of Health, who invented this reading method for blind people, as well as reflective 'cat's eyes' for roadways, and fluorescent armbands for children.

CANT
pious jargon

(a) Named after Emanuel Kant (1877–1936), philosopher, revolutionary, genius and the most boring preacher in Germany.

(b) Named after Cant Stupla Vinyou (1877–1936), Hindu mystic, who once lectured his followers for eleven days, stopping only to eat a goat.

(c) Named after Andrew Cant (1590–1663), Aberdonian Presbyterian minister, whose congregation could not understand a word he was saying.

CLERIHEW
a four-lined humorous verse that does not scan

(a) Named after Edmund Clerihew Bently (1875–1956), who invented this verse-form when he was a schoolboy in London. A detective story writer, Bently became a journalist on the *Daily Telegraph*.

(b) Named after Clerihew Rourke (1741–1838), Irish playwright who began the tradition of kissing the Blarney Stone. He later married Stonehenge.

(c) Named after Suzanne Clerihew (1951–), dyslexic, South African born, certified lunatic, Ms Clerihew works for the *Sun* 'newspaper'.

KILROY WAS HERE
graffiti

(a) Named after an unrecorded American shipyard inspector, who chalked this message to warn steelworkers that he was keeping an eye out for any slackers. American forces brought this message to British walls during World War Two.

(b) Named after Leonard Kilroy (1903–47), a celebrated petty criminal who occupied most of His Majesty's prisons at one time or another, and had a compulsion to leave his mark on any and every blank space of wall. When he escaped from Pentonville in 1937, prisoners used the slogan to annoy their guards.

(c) Named after Professor Kilroy, the hero of H G Wells' astounding novel *The Time Machine*, (1898). Kilroy set out from Victorian London, witnessed the First, Second and Third World Wars, and travelled far into the future to a time when mankind breeds human beings for food. On his return nobody believed his stories. Only his signature remains as a future testimony.

LIMERICK
There was an Old Man who said 'Hush!
I perceive a young bird in this bush!'
When they said – 'Is it small?'
He replied –'Not at all!
It is four times as big as the bush!'

Lear

(a) Named after Stephen Foyle, Third Earl of Limerick (1786–1841), whose idiotic poetry was lampooned by Byron.

(b) Named after Edward Lear (1812–88). The five-lined nonsense poem appeared in his *Book of Nonsense* (1846). 'Learick' was a word coined by Father Mathew Russell.

(c) Named after Old Limericke, an Erse figure, whose abode was a waste piece of ground outside the town, where epic poems were recited.

MALAPROPISM
unwitting misuse of words

(a) Named after the Reverend W A Malaprop (1844–1930), Warden of New College Oxford, who possibly does not deserve his reputation. According to the Reverend James Adderley in 1916, Malaprop only committed such a blunder once, when he brought the house down during a sermon by referring to 'Kinkering Kongs'.

(b) Named after Mrs Malaprop, an eccentric character in Dickens' *The Old Curiosity Shop* of 1875. Literally from *mala propar*, she was wont to talk about such things as 'Kongs on the banks of the Nile'.

(c) Named after Mrs Malaprop, an eccentric character in Sheridan's *The Rivals* of 1775. Literally from *mal à propos* she was wont to talk about such things as 'an allegory on the banks of the Nile'.

MORSE CODE
communication system of dots and dashes

(a) Named after Samuel Hurricane Morse (1691–1772), the most foul-mouthed member of parliament ever to pollute the benches of the House of Commons. His speeches were so disgusting that Hansard had to delete one word in four, replacing them with dots and dashes.

(b) Named after Samuel Breeze Morse (1791–1872). Son of a clergyman, Morse studied fine art and went on to become the founder of the National Academy of Design of the USA. He was honoured for his telegraphic pioneering by Napoleon III.

(c) Named after Samuel Windy Morse (1891–1972). Morse was jailed in Alcatraz for the hideous 'jelly bean murders' of 1934. While in solitary confinement he invented this method of communication by tapping out his messages on the steam pipes of the prison.

MUMBO-JUMBO
incomprehensible ritual, bullshit

(a) Named after the guardian spirit, god protector of the village of the Mandingo tribe of Western Sudan, much celebrated by James Mason, Susan George, and railway bookstalls.

(b) Named after Mama Jumbo (1888–1936), generous, huge murderess and wife of 'Green' Willy. Between them they pulped sixty-seven tax-payers just for kicks during the New Orleans Massacres, but were never convicted due to Mama Jumbo's linguistic prowess.

(c) Named after Air Commodore George 'Mumble Jumbo' Hicks (1884–1917). Incompetent strategist, whose bad judgement led to the death of many young fliers during the First World War.

REUTERS
news agency

(a) Named after Daniel 'Scoop' Reuters in 1915, fearless American reporter who was killed helping the wounded in Flanders.

(b) Named after Paul Julius Reuter in 1851, as a trust for honest reporting in Australia, New Zealand and Britain.

(c) Named after Claude Grandville Reuter in 1896, a notorious gossip, who was unable to keep any confidence.

SPOONERISM
accidental transposition of initial syllables, as in: 'on cooking the first hero of spring . . .' and 'A Sale of Two Titties' by Darles Chickens . . .'

(a) Named after Reverend W A Spooner (1844–1930), Warden of New College Oxford, who possibly does not deserve his reputation. According to the Reverend James Adderley in 1916, Spooner only committed such a blunder once, when he brought the house down during a sermon by referring to 'Kinkering Kongs'.

(b) Named after Mr Spooner, lawyer and verbal gymnast, who appears in *The Pickwick Papers* by Charles Dickens. He is the legal adviser to Mrs Bardell in the misunderstood case of Bardell v Pickwick.

(c) Named after Tom Spooner, one of Robin Hood's band of Merrie Men, and would-be betrayer of his comrades. He was hanged by the Sheriff of Nottingham for spoonerizing the name Friar Tuck.

TACITURN
habitually silent and uncommunicative

(a) Named after Father Ricard Tacitur (1386–1441), founder of the Order of the Silent Brethren at Babel Abbey, Kilmarnockshire. The great and good man died on a visit to his cousin in Cheltenham of a ruptured bladder, unable to ask for the toilet.

(b) Named after Bob Tacit, the surly gardener in William Goldsmith's *Lady Antonia's Fan*. Tacit does not utter one intelligible word throughout the play, despite being a key character.

(c) Named after Publius Cornelius Tacitus (AD 55?–120). A gifted prose stylist and Roman historian, Tacitus was the author of the schoolboy tortures known as *The Histories* and *The Annals*.

THE HUMAN CONDITION

ACHILLES HEEL
vulnerable tendon

(a) Named after Humberto Achilles (1875–1950), shoe manufacturer and designer of the 'stiletto' heel. Achilles has broken more ankles, ruined more floors and lacerated more dancing partners than any man in the history of footwear.

(b) Named after Achilles, Greek warrior. His mum dipped him in the river Styx when he was a lad to make him invulnerable, holding him by one heel. Unfortunately this is exactly where an arrow caught him during the battle for Troy.

(c) Named after Achilles Andrews, the ventriloquist's dummy and tormentor of Peter Brough. Achilles' foot fell off during the Royal Variety Command Performance of 1958.

ADAM'S APPLE
lump in the throat

(a) Named after Adam Smith (1690–1753), pioneering agriculturalist and social theorist.

(b) Named after Adam Faith, alias Terry Nelhams (1941–), actor and teenage heart-throb, whose early pop songs employed his celebrated glottal stop.

(c) Named after Adam, image of God, first man on earth. But did he have a navel?

ADONIS
muscular, beautiful man

(a) Named after Adonis, a mythological Greek youth. Adonis was endowed with great beauty, and was loved to distraction by Aphrodite.

(b) Named after Albert Donis (1902–58). Superbly formed, Mr Donis exhibited himself in and around Manchester between the wars.

(c) Named after Adonysius, an intimate of Plato. Adonysius supposedly fell in love with his own image, which was reflected in a pool of water, and drowned.

CAESAREAN
childbirth by extraction through the abdomen

(a) Named after Augustus Caesareas (1314–72), Venetian anatomist, who painstakingly worked with goats and pigs before attempting these operations on women. It is said that on many occasions he saved both mother and child, whereas it was normal at this time for one or other to be sacrificed.

(b) Named after Julius Caesar (102–44 BC), who was brought into this world by the sword, and removed from it by the dagger.

(c) Named after *Little Caesar* (1930), the first gangster talking picture, the central character of which tires of waiting for the birth of his son, and hurries things along.

FALLOPIAN TUBES
the female oviducts

(a) Named after Fallopia, the Minoan snake goddess and self-fertilized mother of an army of immortal warriors.

(b) Named after Gregory Fallopian (1726–80), the Walloon vivisector, who pioneered prenatal diagnosis of the living from first hand research into the dead.

(c) Named after Gabriello Fallopia (1523–62), alias Fallopio, alias Fallopius, the diligent Italian anatomist who discovered the function of these organs.

GARGANTUAN
giant proportions, especially of appetite

(a) Named after Gargantua, a benign Celtic giant, used by Rabelais in his bawdy satire in 1534. As a child he needed the milk of 17,913 cows for breakfast, and on one occasion ate six pilgrims in a salad.

(b) Named after Gargan Tuan (1895–1936), thirty-four stones of Japanese Sumo wrestler, who trained on vast quantities of blubber, and wrote the moving autobiography, *Whale Meat Again*.

(c) Named after Gargantua, the Roman goddess of plenty, whose followers indulged in sickening gluttony, sometimes leading to death by explosion.

GOLIATH
a giant

(a) Named after Gordon O'Liath (1702–96), well-endowed and popular pugilist and poet, father of seventeen and mother of two.

(b) Named after Norman Goliath (1884–1929), according to medical records the tallest man who ever lived, at ten feet four inches. He enjoyed dancing the fox-trot with women of approximately five feet eleven inches in height.

(c) Named after Goliath, the champion of the Philistines, who suffered the boy David's small rocks.

HERCULES
a strong man, also a pile-driver

(a) Named after Hercules, the strongest man in the ancient philosophical pop group, The Descartes Five.

(b) Named after Herakles, a son of Greek supergod Zeus. Herakles invented a system of cleaning horse dung with rivers.

(c) Named after Hercules (1823–90). Billed as the world's strongest man in Phineus T Barnum's travelling extravaganza. Hercules climaxed his act by lifting a fully grown cow.

PANIC
mindless fear

(a) Named after King Panikin (883–937), a minor English king who ruled an area between Somerset and Dorset, and died of a seizure on discovering a flea in his ear.

(b) Named after Captain Paul Etienne Panic (1773–1812). On receiving false information from a spy, he rode after the French army which was advancing on Moscow, with the news that Paris was burning, spreading alarm and confusion. Napoleon had him shot.

(c) Named after Pan, the rural god with hairy legs, from the Greek, 'panikos . . . caused by Pan', and originally meaning mysterious and fearsome countryside noises.

SAINT VITUS DANCE
inability to keep still, illness promoting uncontrolled movement

(a) Named after Vitus Nihilpede, a Carthusian monk who attempted to dance away the sins of the world in 1317. He danced in frenzied extremes for seventeen weeks from Gosport to Lymington, before joining the Franciscans.

(b) Named after Vitus, Sicilian prince of the fourth century AD, the patron saint of dancers and Saxony, who was martyred in Rome by Diocletian. His name is invoked against certain illnesses, notably cholera.

(c) Named after Saint Vitus, who was made to dance on hot coals and then martyred on a great spiked wheel by the Emperor Maximus.

STENTORIAN
very loud voiced

(a) Named after Stentor, a Greek herald of the Trojan war, who was cursed with a voice as loud as fifty men.

(b) Named after Giacomo Stentorinia (1877–1923), Italian baritone, who battered eardrums three blocks away from the opera house.

(c) Named after Regimental Sergeant Major C J Stentor (1902–61), bull-necked, wax-moustached, he was often used in army recruiting propaganda, for reasons best known to the Ministry of Defence.

TICH

an affectionate rather than abusive nickname for a small person

(a) Named after Harry Relph, 'Little Tich' (1868–1928), the music hall entertainer. In 1866 the Tichbourne Case caught the public imagination, when a little fat Australian claimed to be the missing heir to a fortune. He was jailed for perjury. Harry Relph, a little fat baby, was dubbed Little Tich, and retained the name throughout his life.

(b) Named after Annabelle Leigh Titcher (1802–41), who was exhibited throughout Europe and the United States as the smallest woman in the world. Perfectly formed in every part and quite mature, Titcher measured only eighteen and a half inches in her bare feet.

(c) Named after Tisch (c 1924–45), a pygmy hippopotamus, resident of the Berlin Zoo. A great favourite with the Berliners, Tisch was killed by Russian artillery during the fall of Berlin, and allegedly eaten by person or persons unknown.

A DOZEN MEANS OF TRANSPORT

BLACK MARIA
police vehicle for transporting malcreants

(a) Named after *The Murder of Maria Marten*, a very popular Victorian melodrama of the 1840s, based on an actual case, for which a man was hanged in 1828.

(b) Named after the first ever moving-film studio, built in 1893 for Thomas Edison by Laurie Dickson. Painted matt black both inside and out, it was mounted on a revolving platform so that it could follow the path of natural sunlight.

(c) Named after Maria, a formidable proprietress of a Boston brothel. In the latter part of the nineteenth century, the good lady tirelessly aided police by stuffing obnoxious customers into the barred van.

CHRYSLER
multinational runabout

(a) Named after Walter Percy Chrysler (1875–1951). Manager of the Buick Motor Company from Pittsburgh, Chrysler then worked for General Motors before setting up competition in 1923.

(b) Named after Laurelei Chrysler (1875–1951), Belgian heiress who was infatuated by cars. She raced them, designed them, built them, and was killed in one.

(c) Named after Rusty Chrysler (1875–1951), Detroit comedian and fast-food eliminator.

DIESEL
compression-ignition internal combustion engine

(a) Named after Gottlieb Diesel (1826–88), the eldest son of a Potsdam foundryman. Diesel installed his first engine in a gearless tricycle in 1865, and was immediately offered the backing of the Karl Benz works in Berlin.

(b) Named after Walter Wankel Diesel (1865–1936). An engineer attached to the Max Plank Institute, whose prototype engine was fabricated in 1909. With the rise of Nazism, Diesel emigrated to America, where he died a manic depressive.

(c) Named after Rudolph Diesel (1858–1913), who was born in Paris. He got the backing of Krupps, and built his engine in 1897. Diesel vanished from the face of the earth en route to England and his body was never found.

FOKKER
most famous German fighter aircraft of the First World War

(a) Named after Heinrich Leopold Fokker (1890–1939), six foot four inches of Prussian engineer, who built his prototype with his own hands, and achieved the first recorded loop-the-loop in his tough little aircraft.

(b) Named after Jumbo 'Silly' Fokker (1890–1939), the shy designer of this brilliant aircraft, who lent the plans to a man outside the War Ministry named Schmidt.

(c) Named after Anthony Fokker (1890–1939), a Dutchman who liked England, set up a warplane factory for Germany, and became a US citizen.

HANSOM
horsedrawn cab, taxi

(a) Named after Joseph Hansom (1803–82), the English architect, who designed his safety cab in 1834, one year after completing Birmingham Town Hall.

(b) Named after Albina 'Handsome' Gucci (1882–1932), Colerado icon salesman, who set up the first motorized hire-a-cab business in 1905 and was assassinated during the short, bloody Taxi War.

(c) Named after Paul Luscius Hansom (1857–1941), London coach-builder and inventor of the fold-away roof, he constructed his famous cab in 1886.

JUGGERNAUT
monstrous lorry

(a) Named after John G J 'Rubber Duck' Juggerner (1906–61), Detroit Truckers' Union boss, who paid no heed to law or life in order to get his cargo through. Tragically run over by a Honda moped.

(b) Named after Jagannath, an ancient Hindu god. Hysterical devotees would fling themselves under the wheels of his giant processional statue, to be pulped in suicidal devotion, despite government health warnings.

(c) Named after Richard Bosch Jugger, German designer of the early tank and armoured personnel carrier, and inventor of the caterpillar track.

PHAETON
horse-drawn passenger vehicle

(a) Named after Phaeton, son of the Greek sun god Helios, who stole his father's chariot and drove it without due care and attention.

(b) Named after C J Phaeton (1786–1842), a coachbuilder active in Nantes. He invented a leaf-spring system which separated the passenger compartment from the chassis of the vehicle, which is still used today in several types of automobile.

(c) Named after Phineas T Phaeton (1803–83), a Shropshire eccentric who lived with a family of nine and several dogs in a mail coach.

PUFFING BILLY
steam railway engine

(a) Named after William Hedley, a British engineer, who in 1813 built his railway locomotive slightly before George Stevenson completed his more famous Rocket.

(b) Named after William the Conqueror (1027–84), who became enraged at not receiving an invitation from his friends the Cohens, and threatened to send them a barrel of bear-grease in retaliation.

(c) Named after Billy Bunter, fat owl of the Remove, and devious breathless glutton, in the Greyfriars stories of Frank Richards.

PULLMAN
luxurious railway cabin, often incorporating dining car and sleeping accommodation

(a) Named after Vanessa, Baroness Pullman (1876–1959). Overdressed socialite and spoiled lady, pampered with a private railway carriage which became a mobile party, running around southern France.

(b) Named after William Joel Pullman (1881–1933), failed US presidential candidate. He campaigned in his own railway train, which boasted a sauna, music room and a golf course.

(c) Named after George Mortimer Pullman (1831–97). He patented the Pullman sleeping car in 1864, and was a successful cabinet-maker as well as a versatile American inventor.

RENAULT
French mass-production motor car

(a) Named after Renée Renault (1903–74), vindictive canner of sauced fish, who forced many thousand members of the public into an all-purpose vehicle, which he called Le Hatchback de Notre Dame.

(b) Named after Louis Renault (1877–1950). The Parisian who in 1898 invented the first direct coupling of an engine with the back axle, in 1905 ran the first taxis on the streets of Paris, and in 1907 installed the first air-cooled aircraft engine.

(c) Named after Wankel Renault (1860–1972). Born in Nimes, Renault began manufacturing shovels in 1883, bicycles in 1889, motor cycles in 1904, automobiles in 1911, aircraft in 1920, missiles in 1948, and pet-me wet-me dolls in 1960.

TAXI
passenger transport for hire

(a) Named after Tom Taxey (1477–1549), London ferry boatman, who plied the same stretch of river between Chelsea and Hampton Court for fifty years, and who was patronized by commoner and nobleman alike.

(b) Named after Johan Baptista von Taxis (?–1541), the nephew of a German prince who established a regular postal service between Vienna and Brussels. He made a fortune, and the Taxis family retained the office of Postmaster General for over 300 years, until 1867.

(c) Named after Cab Taxi (1813–70), belligerent sedan chair operator of Bath. Accused of murder, he invented the pedometer while awaiting trial.

ZEPPELIN
cigar-shaped airship

(a) Named after Graaf Spee von Zeppelin (1838–1917), the first man ever to achieve controlled flight, by means of a ribbed rudder attached to his gondola which was slung beneath a balloon. Directional power was supplied by a prototype diesel engine in 1889.

(b) Named after Count Graf Ferdinand von Zeppelin (1838–1917). The Count was involved in the American Civil War to end all wars. He invented the air raid.

(c) Named after Sir Harry Sopwith Zeppelin (1838–1917), whose dirigible aircraft was filled with lighter-than-air gas, and forward motion was provided by sixteen trained swans.

typecasts

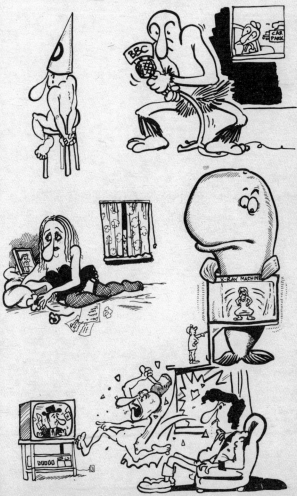

DUNCE
dimwit

(a) Named after Julius John Dunce (1618–1702), a shrewd manipulator and intriguer. Dunce maintained his position in governmental circles through many troubled reigns, by pretending to be a bumbling, harmless idiot.

(b) Named after John Gregory D'Ince (1787–1839), an inarticulate, slobbering degenerate, and member of parliament for the last eighteen years of his pathetic life.

(c) Named after John Duns Scotus (1265–1308), born at Duns, Scotland. He was a Franciscan who opposed and obstructed the teachings of Thomas Aquinas. Contemporaries labelled him a pedant and a blockhead.

GOON
dolt, harmless loony

(a) Named after the Goons, grunting apemen who inhabited a remote desert island, wielding clubs and dragging their knuckles on the ground, as featured in the 1930s cartoons of Popeye the Sailor.

(b) Named after a Second World War nickname, used by British prisoners of war for their German camp guards.

(c) Named after the radio characters of the 1950s comedy broadcasts, created by Spike Milligan, Peter Sellers, Harry Secombe, Michael Bentine and Valentine Dyal.

JONAH
unlucky person, who brings such luck to others.

(a) Named after Jonah, the biblical prophet from Tyre. Many travails were sent to him to test his faith, and he eventually found sanctuary in the belly of a whale before finding favour with God and becoming a tax gatherer.

(b) Named after Zoltan Jonah (?–1926). A would-be bank robber, Jonah never attained his end, due to a loud voice from heaven which always tipped off police, usually reversing the charges.

(c) Named after Jonah, as featured in the *Old Testament, Second Book of Kings, ch 14*. Having disobeyed his god to order the people of Nineveh to repent, he fled the city to the sea, only to be the cause of mass-vomiting.

LUDDITE
a craftsman hostile to machinery replacing man

(a) Named after Lobby Ludd (1904–83), the mystery man of the *News Chronicle*, who gave away five-pound-notes to holiday makers who correctly challenged him. Ludd was replaced by a bingo card, and the newspaper was strike-bound for seven months.

(b) Named after Ludmilla Tereshckova (1888–1937). 'Red Ludmilla' organized the smashing of the Tzar's factories in St Petersburg. She was liquidated by Josef Stalin, who was allegedly envious of her moustache.

(c) Named after Ned Ludd in 1811, known as King Ludd, the organizer against redundancy by machinery in the British textile industry. Spreading from Nottingham across most of industrial England, revolution was averted by harsh repression and mass hangings.

MAUDLIN
tearfully emotional, foolishly drunk

(a) Named after Monty Modlyn (1942–), popular un-popular journalist and broadcaster, and the host of radio phone-in programmes.

(b) Named after Reginald Maudling (1919–1979), popular unpopular businessman and former cabinet minister, with a host of interesting litigation behind him.

(c) Named after Mary Magdalen, who sat by the sepulchre of Jesus between his burial and the resurrection. She has often been depicted in paintings with red-rimmed, tearful eyes.

MAVERICK
stumblebum, attractive rootless rogue

(a) Named after a television cowboy hero, as portrayed by James Garner in the early 1960s. Maverick was a clean-shaven, muscular card-sharp, whose best line of defence was a kissable lip and a spontaneous gun.

(b) Named after Mr Maverick, a Texan active around 1845–56. Maverick was a civil engineer and a difficult neighbour. He owned so many cattle that several were never branded with his mark, which led his henchmen to claim all unbranded cows for Maverick.

(c) Named after Elton 'Nutter' Maverick (1887–1940), manager of the Empire Pool, Wembley. He promoted honest-to-goodness fixed fights for the benefit of his family, George Raft and Edward VII. Maverick was arrested for extortion in 1940, but died during one of the first air raids over London, before coming to trial.

NOSEY PARKER
busybody, spy

(a) Named after Mathew Parker (1504–75). English scholar and prelate, Parker did not have a particularly big nose but it is certain that he stuck it into other people's business.

(b) Named after Frederick Spon Parker (1862–1927). Insidious Home Office adviser. Parker had fascist tendencies and advocated that government dossiers be kept on all 'potential criminals, bolsheviks, Jews and freemasons' in the United Kingdom.

(c) Named after Sir Charles Douglas Parker (1689–1746). This Scottish poet is said to have been the inspiration for Cyrano de Bergerac. The unfortunate Parker's nose was over five and a half inches long.

PEEPING TOM
a domestic spy, often a voyeur

(a) Named after Thomas the Apostle, who could not believe in the resurrection of Jesus unless he saw the Christ, wounds and all, with his own eyes.

(b) Named after Tom the Tailor of Coventry. In 1040 he was the only person to peek at Lady Godiva as she rode naked, in protest against taxes levied on the townsfolk by her husband Leofric. Legend has it that Tom was struck blind.

(c) Named after Thomas Flasher (1794–1837), the Bristol pervert, who was eventually hanged after a lengthy series of unsavoury incidents involving Canadian bananas.

TEDDY BOY
working class, rock'n'rolling snappy dresser

(a) Named after King Edward VII (1848–1910), who was notorious for energetic dancing, drinking, and dressing in bright colours. He sported long jackets with suede lapels, and wore pastel shaded socks.

(b) Named after Senator Edward Kennedy (1926–), overweight politician, who was notorious for energetic dancing, drinking and killing his girlfriends in car accidents. His duck arse hairstyle and crepe soled shoes were widely imitated in the 1950s.

(c) Named after Ted Rogers (1926–) British comedian and founder member of the Elvis Presley Fan Club. Ted still wears the full rig every Friday night.

19 PLACES TO GO ON HOLIDAY...

ALICE SPRINGS
central Australian town

(a) Named after Alice Todd, the wife of Sir Charles Todd, in 1872. The township sprang from the site of a telegraph line interchange, at the centre of the Australian continent.

(b) Named after Alice Kelly-Peters (1864–1913). Three times mayoress of Middle Springs township, the first woman in the continent to be so elected, the inhabitants changed its name in her honour.

(c) Named after 'Red' Alicia Bains, (?–1904). Over six feet tall with auburn hair to her waist, she was a celebrated soprano who retired to this remote settlement.

AMERICA
large land mass to the west of Ireland

(a) Named after Olaf Jamarik (AD fifth century), a Viking warrior who brought back stories of a great frozen continent to Leif Erickson. It is probable that Jamarik had found Greenland, and not America.

(b) Named after Americus, Roman spirit of the setting sun, who married the goddess of commerce, Cola.

(c) Named after Amerigo Vespucci in 1501. A Florentine employed by the King of Spain, Amerigo challenged the authority of Columbus, and sailed southwards from the West Indies. He published his discoveries in *Mondus Novus*.

DELAWARE
American state

(a) Named after Walter Delaware (1772–1831), Secretary of State to Abraham Lincoln, and founder of the New York Philharmonic Quartet.

(b) Named after Thomas West, Twelfth Baron De La Ware (1577–1618). Founder and governor of Virginia in 1610, De La Ware was thrown into prison for complicity in the ill-fated Essex Rebellion.

(c) Named after Deluwar, semi-mythical tribal chief of the Mohican Indians, usually depicted as having the head of a buffalo.

EVEREST
highest mountain peak on this planet

(a) Named after Gilbert Everest (1841–1916), the leader of the first expedition ever mounted to climb this peak. The expedition got as far as Le Havre, where Everest passed away during a long delay at customs.

(b) Named after Sir George Everest (1790–1866). Born in Brecknockshire, Everest was Geographical Surveyor in India from 1816 to 1843, and it was he who fixed the mountain's position and altitude. A critic at the time observed; 'Thank God that his name isn't Shufflebottom.'

(c) Named after Han-Sikin, translated as Everest, the Tibetan equivalent of the Angel of Death. It was believed that no man could ascend the mountain and live, and that even passing through its great shadow was to be avoided.

GRIMSBY
port commanding the Humber estuary

(a) Named after Peiter Grimes (1127–1204). 'Grimes Bay' was the fishing port founded in 1186 by this wild half-Danish captain.

(b) Named after Grim, the masked Norse god, who appeared to mortals in various disguises. He was better known as Odin.

(c) Named after Jos Grimsby (1532–91), where he fell, finally and tragically, fatally choking on a braised seal.

JUPITER
sixth planet, with spots

(a) Named after Jove Optimus Maximus, Roman supergod, who married his sister and laughed a lot.

(b) Named after Jupetto, the carpenter creator of Pinnochio. The fairy story goes back to ancient Greek mythology, wherein Jupetto created the first man from a piece of wood.

(c) Named after Saint Peter, or Jew Peter (AD?–36), first Pope, crucified upside down by the Romans as a terrorist rabble rouser.

MAGINOT LINE
illusionary protection

(a) Named after Monsieur Henri Maginot (1877–1932), the French Minister of Defence who forgot to extend his 'Maginot Line' of defence to the coast. In 1915 the

German army ignored the massive defence system entirely, and simply bypassed it.

(b) Named after Monsieur André Maginot (1897–1952), the French Minister of Defence who forgot to extend his 'Maginot Line' of defence to the coast. In 1940 the German army ignored the massive defence system entirely, and simply bypassed it.

(c) Named after Monsieur Arthur Maginot (1877–1952), the French Minister of Defence who employed exclusively English staff in every restaurant along the German frontier, hoping that the Hun would not tolerate the service and go home.

MARS
fourth planet

(a) Named after Marsbah, Nigerian goddess of chocolate hunting. Toothless and flatulent with sticky fingers, she is experiencing a small revival in Florida.

(b) Named after Mars, father of Romulus and Remus, god of fertility and vegetation and Roman god of war.

(c) Named after Marcelus (?–102 BC), a slave to the Emperor Maximus, who charted the known heavens in his *Ordinians Celestis*.

MERCURY
first planet

(a) Named after Mercurius Gallileo (1372–1440), Italian astronomer and heretic. Gallileo first expounded the theory that it was not the Earth that was the centre of the Solar System.

(b) Named after Marie Curie (1872–1931), pioneer of radiation therapy, to honour her posthumous Nobel Prize for science.

(c) Named after Mercury, the Roman god of thieves and tricksters. He was promoted in 495 B C to god of science, eloquence and the arts, and ended his career as Underworld guide to the dead and patron spirit of travellers.

NEPTUNE
eighth planet

(a) Named after King Neptune (315–247 B C), Phoenician who assembled the first centrally commanded naval fleet in history. Neptune took control of most Mediterranean trade routes and wielded enormous economic power.

(b) Named after Hans Ulrich Neptune (1878–1950). Astronomer and director of the Max Plank Institute, Berlin, Neptune helped develop radio-astronomy which led to the discovery of a planet in 1948.

(c) Named after Neptune, Roman god of making water. Neptune had a rotten temper and would raise a storm or sink a ship with minimal provocation. However, he could be bribed.

PENNSYLVANIA
US territory

(a) Named after Penquanavanea, the mythological father of the Chippawe Indians. Penquanavanea normally manifested himself as a bald eagle, but on occasions was disguised as a silent old man carrying a wooden rod, with which he would point out the direction of game, water, enemies and river fords.

(b) Named after Pena Sylvanus (1621–93), the fanatical Breton nationalist. Disgusted with the degeneracy of French society, Sylvanus founded a self-sufficient community in 1667. Persecuted by the authorities and his neighbours alike, he led his band of two hundred souls to the New World in 1674, to found Pennsylvania.

(c) Named after William Penn (1644–1718), an English Quaker, and the son of Admiral Sir William Penn. He was imprisoned in the Tower of London three times for his preaching, and he set sail in 1682 to found his Quaker colony. Most of the colonists flouted his authority, and he returned to England within two years. He landed in debtors' prison.

PLUTO
ninth planet

(a) Named after Pluto, the Egyptian dog-headed deity, closely associated with the fearsome god Mikhim Ows.

(b) Named after Plutarch (AD 270–329), historian and chronicler of gods and emperors, Shakespeare stole several of Plutarch's plots and characterizations.

(c) Named after Pluto, Greek god of the infernal underworld, and giver of wealth.

RHODESIA
southern African territory

(a) Named after Wilfred Rhodes (1877–1946). A Yorkshire cricketer, Rhodes represented his country for thirty years. At the age of fifty he was dominant in winning the 'Sheffield' Test Match series.

(b) Named after Cecil John Rhodes (1853–1902). The son of a vicar, Rhodes emigrated to South Africa for health reasons. At the age of twenty he envisaged an all-British Africa, and set about buying it up from the tribal chiefs.

(c) Named after Zimbabwe Rhodesi (1864–1929). Powerful leader of his tribe, Rhodesi negotiated the 1896 Native Rights Treaty with the British, which promised the right of all tribesmen to work for their new masters.

SATURN
fifth planet, with rings

(a) Named after Saturnus, Roman god of agriculture, who housed the treasury in his basement, and had his midwinter celebrations stolen by the Christians.

(b) Named after Satan, fallen angel, tipped for the top job before his dispute with Saint Michael. He was cast into outer darkness and became associated with the planet's mysterious rings.

(c) Named after Saturna (?–329 B C), ancient Greek society hostess whose annual end of year party developed into the legendary 'Saturnalia.'

TASMANIA
island territory off the south-east coast of Australia

(a) Named after Admiral Pommy Tasman (1602–59), English explorer and naturalist, whose logbook records an island where the natives had long tails and were able to leap great distances in a hopping motion. Tasman suffered from myopia.

(b) Named after Abel Jenszon Tasman (1602–59), the Dutch explorer who circumnavigated Australia, and discovered Van Diemen's Land in 1642. The island was renamed Tasmania in his honour, in 1853. Tasman was the discoverer of New Zealand and the Fiji Islands.

(c) Named after 'Tazmaniac' (1741–1820), the pseudonym of a member of the British Royal Family, and a forerunner of Tarzan. Tazmaniac was exiled to Botany Bay for swinging on chandeliers in the Palace, and was further exiled by the convicts to an offshore island because of his lack of social graces.

TRISTAN DA CUNHA
celebrated volcanic island

(a) Named after Tristan da Cunha (1460–1540), the Portuguese navigator and explorer of the eastern coast of Africa. He discovered this island in the Atlantic in 1506.

(b) Named after Tristan de Kuhhirt, Wagner's heroic cowherd, who is transformed into a silver bicycle bell in the Ring Cycle.

(c) Named after Tristan Salvarez (1501–79). Born on Cunha island, he predicted the volcanic eruption of 1560, having observed the agitated behaviour of livestock and wild birds, thereby saving his people.

URANUS
seventh planet

(a) Named after Uranus, first ruler of the world, father of the one-eyed cyclops, and of a quartet of children who boasted 100 hands each. Uranus had an unhappy family life; his mum did not know he had been born, and his son cut off his genitals and threw them into the sea.

(b) Named after Uran Bhatur (AD?–817), Mongolian war-lord, and patron of the arts and sciences. He founded the city-state which is the capital of modern Siberia.

(c) The author refuses to make any puerile jokes about arseholes.

VANCOUVER
Canadian island territory

(a) Named after George Vancouver (1758–98), the English navigator. Vancouver sailed under Captain Cook during his circumnavigation of the world, and he was the first man to sail around the island that bears his name. The book of his life's work was completed by his brother.

(b) Named after Louis Louaie Vancouvier (1632–1711), the French explorer. Vancouvier claimed the island for the French throne in 1683. It was annexed by the British twenty years later, at which time Vancouvier lost his head during the French revolution.

(c) Named after Jan van Couver (1780–1849), a Dutch trapper. Van Couver began his career trading in animal furs, until signing trading agreements with the island's six tribal leaders. He organized a workable socialist community for several years, trading tools and cloth for pelts.

VENUS
second planet

(a) Named after Goodshippe Venus (1307–83), alchemist and astronomer royal. Venus correctly stated that the planet went through phases of waxing and waning similar to that of the moon.

(b) Named after Venus, Greek goddess of love, passion and grace.

(c) Named after Venus, Roman goddess of gardens and growth.

...AND
7 TIMES TO
GO THERE

AUGUST
eighth month of the year

(a) Named after Augustres, the Greek spirit of the Autumn wind. She loved all living things but was cursed in that everything she touched withered and died.

(b) Named after Hawkquist (AD ?-872), a Saxon warrior chieftain, who conquered Wessex but settled there in peace as a pastry cook.

(c) Named after Augustus Caesar (63 BC–AD 14), egocentric Emperor of Rome who invited saints Joseph and Mary to Bethlehem, for tax purposes.

FRIDAY
Muslim day of rest

(a) Named after Fria, the Roman goddess, and wife of Zeus, father of all gods.

(b) Named after Frido, the Greek goddess of water, and mistress of several Olympians.

(c) Named after Frig, the Norse goddess, and wife of Woden, the one-eyed master of magic, and god of the dead.

JANUARY
first month of the year

(a) Named after Ianiua, Egyptian three-legged god.

(b) Named after Janus, Roman two-faced god.

(c) Named after Janua, Greek one-eyed goddess.

MARCH
third month of the year

(a) Named after the Emperor Marcus Aurelius (109–60 BC), overthrown by the young Julius Caesar.

(b) Named after Mars, the Roman god of war.

(c) Named after Hervick, Earl of March (1172–1253), Saxon warlord who conquered Wales for the Normans.

SATURDAY
Fats Domino's favourite day

(a) Named after St Turd, patron saint of popular British journalism.

(b) Named after Saturn, Roman god, whose New Year festival, *Saturni dies*, became associated with non-working days.

(c) Named after Satur, a Gaelic mythological figure, depicted as half-man, half-milking stool.

THURSDAY
publishing day of the Beano

(a) Named after Thurst, the Germanic equivalent of Pan, the hooved faun.

(b) Named after Thor, the thunder god, whose mighty hammer struck the skies. He was extremely strong but stupid.

(c) Named after Marcus Lusius Thurstus (72–21 BC), second Roman governor of Britain, who imposed an organized calendar on the primitive Britons.

WEDNESDAY
mid-week day

(a) Named after Luciens Wedens, Pope Gregory III (1211–68), who reorganized the Christian calendar in the year 1262.

(b) Named after Woden, the one-eyed master of magic, and god of the dead. This demanding deity required human sacrifice to keep him happy.

(c) Named after King Widnes (AD?–658), the remarkable leader of the Wessex tribes, who defeated the Danes near Chichester in AD 642.

STRENGTHS AND WEAKNESSES

BOYCOTT

to refuse to have any dealings with an individual or an entire nation, for reasons of outrage and/or expediency. First used in the Daily News *13 December 1880*

(a) Named after Lady Alwen Boycott (1851–98). The good lady's husband owned rented property in Whitechapel, which was so disgusting that Lady Boycott wrote to the *Daily News* stating that until he 'protects the tenants against the elements and eliminates the vermin' she would withdraw her sexual favours. Public opinion fell into opposing camps of social reformers and traditionalists. The Whitechapel tenants did not benefit in the slightest.

(b) Named after Cecil Henry Boycott (1822–80). Whilst serving for the East India Company in Bombay, Boycott fell in love with and married a young woman who was beautiful, thirty years his junior and dark brown. The British expatriot community were shocked at this liaison, and Boycott was harassed in every aspect of his work and social life. He shot his wife one evening after tea, and committed suicide over her body.

(c) Named after Captain Charles Cunningham Boycott (1832–97). A bald dwarf with a long white beard, Boycott was a land agent in County Mayo, whose oppressed tenants refused to work for him and stopped him from getting any provisions locally. He finally gathered in his own crops with fifty Orangemen, nine hundred soldiers and two field guns.

CABAL
clique, secret group

(a) Named after Edith Cabal (1874–1917), the English nurse working in war-torn France. She was shot by the Germans as a spy, to the horror of the English newspaper-reading public.

(b) Named after Alistair Crowley Cabal (1382–1451), satanist and pervert. Founder of the Cabalistic Symbolic Rituals and the Black Mass, Cabal was burned at the stake in Cambridge.

(c) Named after the initials of a prototype cabinet, gathered together by King Charles II in 1672. Comprising Lord Clifford, Lord Arlington, the Duke of Buckingham, Lord Ashley and the Duke of Lauderdale.

FABIAN
evolutionary socialism

(a) Named after 'Fabian of the Yard', 1950s television series that featured a proletarian Chief Inspector determined to smash the corruption in the ruling classes of post-war Britain.

(b) Named after Jocelyn Hubert Fabian (1821–1913), founder of the 'Fabian Society' in 1883, with George Bernard Shaw, Sidney Webb and H G Wells.

(c) Named after Quintus Fabius Maximus (232–196 BC), Roman dictator who invented successful guerilla warfare when he defeated Hannibal's army without meeting in open battle.

GERRYMANDER

to arrange electoral boundaries in such a way as to give unfair advantage to a particular candidate

(a) Named after Gerald 'Gerry' Maunder MP (1792–1870), who hung on to the 'rotten borough' of Old Sarum for thirty years, while there were only seven electors living in the constituency, whilst nearby Maybridge-Southampton had 25,000 unrepresented inhabitants.

(b) Named after Horatio Gerrymander (1882–1939), Chief Cartographer at Ordnance Survey, Maybush, Southampton, who during the 1933 local elections falsified official boundary lines, in support of the British Fascist Party.

(c) Named after Elbridge Gerry (1744–1824), Governor of Massachusetts, whose distortion of the 1812 Essex County boundary looked like the outline of a salamander. A local master of wit at the time quipped 'better say a gerrymander'.

HIPPOCRATIC OATH

doctor's code

(a) Named after Hippocrates, a fifth century BC Greek physician who invented a wine filtering system made out of a woollen sock.

(b) Named after Hippocratus (AD 55–113), Roman doctor who first tabulated a charter of medical ethics, along with a scale of fees.

(c) Named after Dave 'Hippo' Crater (1880–1961), New Zealand boxer whose leisure time was engaged in swearing at surgeons.

HOBSON'S CHOICE
no choice at all

(a) Named after Thomas Hobson (1544–1631), equine renter whose customers always had to hire the horse that stood nearest to the stable door. Hobson was celebrated in verse by Milton, and has a Cambridge street named after him.

(b) Named after the central character in Harold Brighthouse's comedy of the same name, in which a tyrannical father gets his come-uppance. It has been filmed in a 1920 silent version, a 1931 sound remake, and in David Lean's superb 1954 production with Charles Laughton.

(c) Named after Henry Ford's production manager on the 'Model T' assembly line, Rheingold Hobson (1878–1942). His famous quotation, 'You can have a model T in any colour, so long as it's black,' is wrongly attributed to Ford himself.

HYGIENE
next to godliness

(a) Named after Hygiena, the daughter of Asclepius, god of healing. This lady personified health, cleanliness and was a very good insurance risk.

(b) Named after Anton Fester Hygiene (1731–1826). Inventor of the enclosed sauna bath, Hygiene washed his body on the hour, every hour, from top to toe. He eventually puckered to death.

(c) Named after Claude Halle Hygiena (1847–1924). The pioneer of modern kitchen design, his storage units, worktops and preparation modules advanced efficiency and retarded architectural innovation in the domestic kitchen for two generations.

MARXISM

from each according to his means, to each according to his needs

(a) Named after Julius Marx, alias Groucho (1890–1977), philosopher, writer and comic, who made nations laugh.

(b) Named after S M Marks (1898–   ), who with his partner Spencer, and without prejudice, clothes both indigenous British and visiting Arabic proletariat, under the banner of Saint Michael.

(c) Named after Karl Marx (1818–83), a nice Jewish boy, and lover of real ale. From the age of thirty-one until his death, Karl lived in London, contributing to Putnam's weekly and changing the future of the entire planet.

ONANIST

male masturbator, wanker

(a) Named after Decimus Onanus (AD 72–136), Roman Senator who often practised his little weakness during public mass debates.

(b) Named after Luigi Onano (1640–1708), a blind Italian who suffered from bad skin and unaccountable hairy palms. He died insane and tired.

(c) Named after Onan, son of Judah, who refused to have sexual intercourse with a certain woman. However, if *Genesis ch. XXXVIII, vs 7–10* is accurate, it is unfair to accuse him of self-abuse.

SPARTACISTS
German extreme socialists, 1920s

(a) Named after Karl Marx (1818–83), alias Spartacus, the pen name he used when contributing to Putnam's weekly magazine.

(b) Named after Spartacus (?–71 BC), a Thracian shepherd, taken by Romans as a slave, who became a gladiator. In 73 BC he escaped with seventy others to the crater of Vesuvius, from where he raised an army of over 100,000 men, before his final defeat at the hands of Crassus.

(c) Named after H Klauswitz Spartacos (1896–1934), the Berlin doctor of philosophy. He opposed Hitler and the rise of Nazism from the very beginning, and advocated any means to stop their progress, no matter if innocent people were killed in the process, or democratic means were ignored.

TONTINE
annuity collected by the surviving member of a group of subscribers

(a) Named after Marguerita La Comptesse du Tontine, (1577–1653), who declared that her fortune was to be inherited by the last surviving of her eighteen children. The subsequent humour, law suits and two suspected murders were chronicled in *La Tontine, une histoire*, by Dumas the Elder.

(b) Named after Diego Tontin, a Sicilian adventurer, who organized a group of twelve Milanese gentlemen as members of such a scheme in 1760. He was assassinated in 1802 by the two surviving subscribers.

(c) Named after Lorenzo Tonte, an Italian banker, who introduced this system into France in 1653 as a method of insurance, coupled with wagering on longevity.

17 WAYS
TO AMUSE
YOURSELF

CALYPSO
a type of West Indian folk song

(a) Named after Calypso, a Greek nymph who sang to Odysseus for three years, while bearing him three children on her enchanted island. Even her promise of granting him immortality failed to cure his homesickness, and he went home.

(b) Named after Calypso Belafonte (1947–) the daughter of popular singer Harry Belafonte to whom he dedicated the much-loved 'Banana Brat Song'.

(c) Named after Winston F Grant (1926–64), the great Jamaican singer, nicknamed 'Collapso', on account of his habit of falling over mid-performance. Winston's dad owned a rum distillery.

CATHERINE WHEEL
spinning firework

(a) Named after Saint Catherine of Alexandria, who was martyred on a terrible spiked wheel by the Emperor Maximus after she had failed to convert him to christianity.

(b) Named after Catherine of Aragon (1485–1536), who brought the rumbustious dance, the Tarantella, to the court of Henry VIII, and set the English nobility whirling round the ballroom.

(c) Named after Brock Catherine (1846–1905), Wessex fire-work manufacturer, who sold his spinning wheels ·for three a penny.

CHRISTY MINSTREL
vaudeville, black-face-entertainer

(a) Named after Joshua Geldblatt Christy (1873–1931), music master of Al Jolson. Christy invented the popular singing style known as 'Rhythm'n'Jews'.

(b) Named after George Christy (?–1873) by the poet John Ruskin in 1875. Christy was a popular entertainer, famed for his singing of working songs.

(c) Named after Christina Solamonsen (1831–73), the Danish singer and banjo plucker, who worked throughout the Yukon with her whistling dog Nathan.

CRAPPS
dice game

(a) Named after Johnny 'The Toad' Crapard, alias Bernard Marigny, the Frenchman who introduced dice playing to New Orleans at the beginning of the nineteenth century.

(b) Named after Jimmy 'The Aardvark' Crapper, the Scotsman who introduced roulette to London at the beginning of the twentieth century.

(c) Named after Wendy 'The Moron' Crapinski, the kissogram lady who introduced Johnny 'The Toad' to Jimmy 'The Aardvark' at the beginning of evensong in Durham Cathedral.

CRUFTS
annual British doggy bonanza

(a) Named after Charles Cruft (1852–1935). At the age of thirteen Cruft went into the service of James Spratt, dog biscuit manufacturer, and retired at the age of forty-three as its manager. He organized his first dog show in 1886, and did much to improve breeds and popularize dogs.

(b) Named after Snuffles Wuffles Whoopsyplop Crufts (?–1902), a repulsive pekinese bitch, whose name was given to the first all-England canine competition for no better reason than she belonged to a certain Queen Victoria.

(c) Named after Viscount Percival Crufts of Bletchley (1776–1860). The founder of the Battersea Dogs Home, the RSPCA and Crufts Dog Show, he made a fortune from shipping slaves to America.

DIXIELAND
area of the USA, and the jazz music played there

(a) Named after Dix Beiderbeck (1887–1937), the jazz trumpeter and early recording star, whose 'Dixieland Gumboil Stomp' drove an entire generation to the opera.

(b) Named after Jeremiah Dixon, an Englishman, who with his partner Charles Mason surveyed the boundary between Maryland and Pennsylvania in the years 1763–67. The 'Mason-Dixon Line' had become abbreviated to 'Dixie' by 1778.

(c) Named after Mason Dixon (1806–82), first governor of Maryland, who decreed that all negroes would go about playing happy spontaneous music with a natural sense of rhythm, eating fried chicken and watermelon.

DOBRO
guitar using resonating cones instead of a hollow body

(a) Named after Blind Johnny Dobro (?–1943), American negro blues singer, who was too poor to buy a guitar, and made his own from empty soup cans.

(b) Named after Stephen D'Obro (1898–1957), guitarist with Django Reinhardt's Hot Club Quintet in wartime Paris.

(c) Named after the three Czechoslovakian Dopera brothers in 1926. They are still producing their own instruments in the USA.

FERRIS WHEEL
fairground machine, offering cyclic views and making children sick

(a) Named after Saint Ferris, Patron Saint of acrobats, who was martyred by the Emperor Maximus on a great spiked wheel after failing to convert him to Christianity and burning some toast.

(b) Named after Sir William Ferris (1591–1613), governor of Carisbrooke Castle and designer of the charming donkey-powered wheel, used to draw water from a deep well. Ferris was addicted to burnt toast.

(c) Named after George W G Ferris (1859–96), an American railroad engineer and bridge designer. Mr Ferris' monster wheel was first exhibited at the Chicago World Exposition of 1893, near a toast stand.

FRISBEE
leisurely disc throwing

(a) Named after the original legendary American little-old-grey-haired lady and terrible pie-maker, Mother Frisbee, whose pies threw better than they tasted.

(b) Named after Eugene Bunger Frisbee (1900–81), the inventor of the yo-yo, the hula-hoop, clackers, the skate-board, the hydrogen bomb and the frisbee. He died penniless and insane.

(c) Named after Fritz Bach (1921–81), German refugee who fled to America in 1934. He invented the art of spinning and catching old hub caps, in the gutters of New York.

HAM
rotten, exaggerating actor

(a) Named after Hamish McCullogh (1835–85), who toured Illinois with his troupe known as Ham's Actors. His entire company was unspeakably terrible, but grew extremely agile at dodging missiles.

(b) Named after Oscar Hammerstein (1872–1951). Originally a compliment for leading musical comedy actors, the meaning is now reversed.

(c) Named after Ham, son of Noah, who imitated all of the earth's animals *ad nauseam* during the flood.

JOHN PAUL JONES
type of communal dance; wife swapping

(a) Named after Hubert Winklebaum (1921–58), dried fruit wholesaler of 23 Valetta Avenue, Coventry, who organized formation dance contests.

(b) Named after John Paul Jones (1747–92), a Scotsman who killed Englishmen, was a captain in the American navy, an admiral in the Russian navy, and died a Frenchman.

(c) Named after John Paul Jones (1821–58), a philandering socialite who changed his partners more often than his socks.

OSCAR
Hollywood bauble of acclaim

(a) Named after Oscar B Meyer in 1929, who first presented the golden statuettes while head of M G M studios.

(b) Named after Oscar Pierce in 1931, by Mrs Margaret Herrick who was Secretary to the Academy of Motion Pictures. The ten inch round-headed protrusion reminded her of her Uncle Oscar.

(c) Named after Oscar Face in 1927, who originally designed the award in Los Angeles.

ST LEGER
a horse race, run at Doncaster

(a) Named after St Leger, patron saint of equestrians, on whose feast day, 15 September, the race was first run.

(b) Named after William St Leger (1871–1922), a Jersey born playboy, who won Doncaster Race Course playing dice in 1904, and held a race every year to commemorate the event.

(c) Named after Colonel St Leger, of Parkhill, Doncaster, who inaugurated the race in 1776. The first winner was Lord Rockingham's Samson.

SAXOPHONE
musical instrument, utilizing a vibrating reed modified by a keyed horn

(a) Named after Antoine Joseph Sax (1814–94), a Belgian who preferred to be known as Adolph. He invented the saxhorn in 1842, the saxotromba in 1845 and the saxophone in 1846.

(b) Named after Charles Joseph Sax (1791–1865), a Belgian musicologist and instrument-maker, who improved the harp, bass-clarinet, guitar and piano, and invented the saxophone in 1861.

(c) Named after Adolph Louis Sax (1860–1923), a founder member of the Original Dixieland Jazzband, of New Orleans. He made over thirty prototypes before patenting his saxophone in 1908.

SOUSAPHONE
giant bass tuba

(a) Named after Sousa, fearsome Celtic spirit of the four winds, who could be appeased by long blasts on ancient curved horns.

(b) Named after Alexei N V Sousakorachinov (1881–1939), pal of Leon Trotsky and the first choreographer of the Red Army Marching Band Latrine Maintenance Division.

(c) Named after John Philip Sousa (1854–1932), the composer of 'The Stars and Stripes Forever' in 1897. He enjoyed his superstar status at home and abroad with obscene gusto.

THESPIAN
actor, player of parts

(a) Named after Saint Thespian, the patron saint of actors, who was martyred by the Emperor Maximus on a terrible spiked wheel after forgetting his lines.

(b) Named after Walter Thespius (1541–1629). Proof now exists to show that it was Thespius who wrote all of Roger Bacon's plays, under the assumed name of Shakespeare.

(c) Named after Thespis (sixth century BC), the Greek poet and father of all play acting. He introduced the actor into the ritual chorus events that were connected with Bacchus worship. The actor was placed on a table and he wore linen masks to interpret different characters. Thespis also invented the prologue and dialogue of Greek drama.

ZIEGFELD GIRL
dancing, singing stage beauty

(a) Named after Florence Ziegfeld (1901–56), trained as a ballet dancer, she caused a sensation in the burlesque halls of the twenties with her liberated dancing and singing style. In 1932 she formed her first corps of Ziegfeld Girls, dominating Broadway for a decade.

(b) Named after Louis B Ziegfeld (1888–1949). A German immigrant to New York at the age of fourteen, Ziegfeld began his working life as unemployable. By the 1920s he was directing his famous musical silent films for MGM.

(c) Named after Florenz Ziegfeld (1869–1932), a fairground barker who made and lost five fortunes during the course of his career. He first produced his Ziegfeld Follies in New York in 1907.

21 LOST PATENTS

BAKELITE
tough artificial plastic

(a) Named after Dr Leo Hendrick Baekeland (1863–1944). He was trying to find a substitute for shellac when he rediscovered phenolic plastic in 1907, thirty-five years after Dr Adolf von Baeyer had first synthesized it. Baekeland also invented photographic paper usable in artificial light.

(b) Named after Dr Henry Baker (1874–1935), who was looking for an artificial tortoiseshell for decorative purposes. In 1920 he discovered by accident that a plastic phenol combined with aldehydes was an excellent electrical insulator.

(c) Named after Dr Irene Megan Bakel (1902–   ), who was experimenting with porcelain substitutes for false teeth manufacture, when she created this plastic in 1940. Bakel also invented non-inflammable safety film.

BIRO
pen utilizing a solidified ink cartridge and a rolling ball tip

(a) Named after Georg Biro (1909–85) in 1938. Biro was a Hungarian inventor who produced a pen which could write through butter while underwater, and costing two hundred dollars.

(b) Named after the initials of the British Imperial Research Office, Salisbury, Wiltshire, where in wartime exiled boffins developed this reliable writing implement for bomber command in 1943. It replaced breakable pencils and leaking, unpressurized fountain pens.

(c) Named after Bryan Biro (1928–77). Aged nineteen, Biro started his business from his stepfather's garage in Wisconsin. Within five years he was a millionaire, with his pens selling throughout the USA at five dollars each. Within fifteen years his pens were selling throughout the world at five cents each, but Biro was bankrupt.

BRAMAH LOCK
safety barrel-lock

(a) Named after Joseph Bramah (1748–1814), the English engineer who patented his safety lock in 1784. Bramah invented a hydraulic press, and became well known for printing his own banknotes.

(b) Named after the Maharajah Pasha Bramah (1714–71), who locked his poor wife into an ingenious chastity belt, which not even he could unlock. He died of tetanus poisoning.

(c) Named after Robert Bramah (1893–1946), Jamaican born clergyman and inventor, who also fabricated a wide range of modesty garments for cattle.

BUNSEN BURNER
laboratory instrument producing a variable gas flame

(a) Named after Wilhelm Bunsen (1811–99), one-eyed professor of chemistry at Heidelberg. Bunsen also invented the photometer and the galvanic battery.

(b) Named after Sir Charles Bunsen (1784–1840), one-armed Fellow of the Royal Society, who brought gas street lighting to many areas of London's West End.

(c) Named after Louis P Bunsen (1851–1921), one-legged physicist at Harvard University. He also invented the vacuum flask and pop-up toaster.

CHUBB LOCK
security lock

(a) Named after Imwar Grand Swetti of Chubb (1317–86), Ottoman potentate and opportunist, who began his career fighting Crusaders and ended it selling them chastity belts for their loved ones.

(b) Named after Mortimer 'Chubby' Yale (1853–1923), grossly fat Delaware mechanic, he introduced his Universal Security Closer in 1897 under the Yale trademark. Because of a patent dispute, the name Chubb was used in Britain.

(c) Named after Charlie Chubb (1772–1845), centre of a family empire of locksmiths in Winchester and London. Chubb perfected fire-proof safes, burglar alarms and window locks.

DAVY LAMP
safety lamp for miners

(a) Named after Sir David Humphrey (1826–98) in 1879. He also introduced the safety innovations of caged birds in the pits. Hung in overhead pockets these birds would collapse if poisonous fumes were present in the mine shaft.

(b) Named after Sir Humphrey Davy (1778–1826) in 1816. Davy was a popular and amusing lecturer, drawing large crowds. This chemist discovered laughing gas, potassium, sodium, chlorine and the demonstration of the true carbon composition of diamonds. He achieved the latter by setting fire to them.

(c) Named after Winifred Davy (1859–1919) in 1903. The wife of a Welsh mine owner, and a founder member of the Fabian Society, she did much to improve the miners' working conditions, lifting them from the disgusting to the miserable.

DERRICK
hoist, lifting device

(a) Named after Eugene Lutyens DeRuyk (1513–71), Dutch inventor of the modern articulated crane, who died of a ruptured bladder whilst looking upwards.

(b) Named after Montague Derrick (1786–1873), associate of Sir Joseph Paxton, who invented a rail-mounted universal hoist which was used in the rapid assembly of the pre-fabricated Crystal Palace.

(c) Named after Black Derrick, who was active around 1600 at Tyburn. Derrick was an accomplished hangman who left his name to the Tyburn gibbet.

GALVANIZE
electrical process of induction, colloquially to prod into action

(a) Named after Umberto Yusek Galvanus (1386–1470), a Venetian alchemist who first postulated the existence of an electrical force. He believed that it was sent to Earth in the form of lightning by angered angels.

(b) Named after Otto 'Sparky' Galvano (1843–1916), the despicable nun smuggler. Galvano was the first man to be publically executed in the electric chair.

(c) Named after Luigi Galvani (1737–98), the Italian physicist. He played with frogs' legs and proposed that it was animal electricity that caused them to twitch.

GILLETTE
safety razor

(a) Named after King Camp Gillette, American inventor, whose hirsute face still appears on the packaging of some blades.

(b) Named after Queen Gay Gillette, Lithuanian hothead who cut her lover's throat with a razor, when he laughed at her armpits.

(c) Named after André Gille, French haemophiliac, paedophiliac, necrophiliac and chef.

HOOVER
a vacuum cleaner

(a) Named after W H Hoover of the Hoover Suction Sweeper Company in 1908. Hoover bought the rights of the device from its wooden-legged inventor J Murray Spangler.

(b) Named after Neville Hoover Chamberlain in 1939, a bit of a sucker.

(c) Named after J Edgar Hoover, tyrannical head of the FBI in 1929. Hoover's method of sweeping gangsters off the streets and beating them senseless reminded the New York public of a cleaning machine.

KELVINATOR
refrigerator, air-conditioner

(a) Named after William Thomson, Baron Kelvin (1824–1907). Born in Belfast, Kelvin matriculated at the age of ten. He advanced telegraphy, perfected over eighty electrical instruments, including the consumer's electricity meter, postulated an atomic theory, created the modern maritime compass and invented the water tap.

(b) Named after Maximillian Heldgrad Kelvin (1852–1907). Born in Vienna, Kelvin matriculated at the age of fifteen. He advanced photography, perfected over twenty electrical instruments including the ammeter, postulated a molecular theory, created the modern draughtsman's compasses, and invented the heat-exchanger.

(c) Named after Melvin Kelvin (1889–1907). Born in Catford, Kelvin matriculated at the age of thirty-six. He advanced to pornography, perfected over three hundred electrical instruments including the battery operated toothbrush, created the modern whoopee cushion and invented the ice cube.

LUCIFER
friction match

(a) Named after Saint Lucia (?–1514), Italian martyr who was burned in Avignon. '*Lucia feu*' was the slang expression used by French soldiers during the Great War, and it was adopted by the British.

(b) Named after Lucifer, the fallen angel, who preferred to be a king amidst the sulphur, than number two in Heaven. The sulphur of the match-head related to the fiery pits.

(c) Named after Lucifer Andreneus (1822–1906), Flemish inventor of the modern friction match in 1901. Before this either tinder boxes were used, or wooden matches tipped with glass beads containing acid.

MONKEY WRENCH
large spanner

(a) Named after Mickey 'The Monkey' Grifford (1876–1945), an infamous London burglar, who gained entry by climbing up walls and over roofs without the aid of ropes or hooks. He invented the adjustable wrench to force open skylights.

(b) Named after Charles Monke in 1856, who aided the rapid growth of the industrial revolution by perfecting nuts, bolts and means to secure them. Before this, hot rivetting was the only means of connecting large machine components.

(c) Named after Compte Phillip D'Aubigny Marque (1683–1740), the original 'Man in the Iron Mask', who was freed by such a device from his shackles.

PASTEURIZE
process of milk sterilization

(a) Named after Pastura, the she-wolf who suckled the abandoned infants Romulus and Remus. Nourished by her milk they grew strong, to become the founders of Rome.

(b) Named after Pastor Peter Paster (1803–1926), the ordained milkman of Peterborough, who mixed his dairy produce with strontium 90, to kill off bacteria.

(c) Named after Louis Pasteur (1822–95), the saviour of the French silk industry, who invented a cure for rabies.

PINCHBECK
counterfeit, spurious: alloy of copper and zinc to imitate gold

(a) Named after King Richard III, who was nicknamed 'Pinchbeck'. In order to bail himself out of political and financial bankruptcy, he had his own treasury melted down and debased.

(b) Named after Christopher Pinchbeck (1670–1732), a London toymaker and watchmaker, who never intentionally used his alloy for purposes of fraud.

(c) Named after Bernard Pinchbeck (1936–   ), Australian-born entrepreneur and convicted swindler, who was at the centre of the Groundnut Mines, or 'Fool's Gold' scandal of 1968.

TARMAC
road surface of small hard stones in mastic

(a) Named after John Loudon Macadam (?–1836), Scots General Surveyor of Roads in England from 1827. In 1819 he published an essay on the method of paving roads with small broken stones.

(b) Named after 'Tar' Mack, a Belfast labourer and former Royal Marine, active in the construction of the Manchester Ship Canal. He was a born innovator, although he could neither read nor write.

(c) Named after Toby Mack (1806–71), Newcastle minerologist, who discovered the Great Asphalt Lake in Trinidad.

TUPPERWARE
party-inducing plastic

(a) Named after Mr Tupper, the mild-mannered house guest in Charles Dickens' *The Pickwick Papers*. Tupper was always too embarrassed to eat at the dining-table, and would take his food from a small lidded box.

(b) Named after Martin Farquhar Tupper (1810–89), indifferent author, mediocre poet and unsuccessful inventor.

(c) Named after Jonas Irving Tupperwalski (1891–1957), American plastics baron, who ordained that he should be buried not in a wooden coffin, but a milky plastic air-proof container, and his cadaver kept in a refrigerator.

VERY LIGHT
pistol-launched, parachute-lowered illumination, normally military

(a) Named after Vera Lynn (1921–   ), the Forces' sweetheart, who lightened our darkness in the terrible days of Nazi menace and 'Two-Way Family Favourites'.

(b) Named after Vaery, the Viking goddess of starlight, and derivation of the middle-English faerie and modern fairy.

(c) Named after Edward Very (1847–1910), US naval officer. Very was an ordnance expert and cartographer. He invented his pistol and light in 1877.

VESTA
match, originally of wax, now of wood

(a) Named after Vesta, the Roman goddess of the blazing hearth, whose nubile young acolytes, the Vestal Virgins, ended the eternal fire which burned inside her temple.

(b) Named after Gerald Swan Vesta (1823–88), matchstick baron. He invented the sliding matchbox, the abrasive striking-strip and the modern 'safety' match. Vesta was burned to death in tragic, if ironic, circumstances.

(c) Named after Vesta Tilley (1847–1920). The famous Victorian music hall star, whose slim figure and volatile temperament reminded her public of a flaming matchstick.

VULCANIZE
rubber processed at high temperature with sulphur

(a) Named after Eberhardt Vulcan (1887–1958), German chemist and industrialist. The Vulcanfabrik at Essen produced cheap, efficient industrial shock-absorbers, and an extremely wide range of marital aids.

(b) Named after Vulcan, the Roman god of fire and metal-working. It is after this god that volcanoes also take their name.

(c) Named after Bengt Soderlund Vulcan (1834–1916), Swedish galoshes manufacturer, whose farsighted research endowments gave the world inflatable boats, weather balloons and washing-up gloves.

WALDO
mechanical hand

(a) Named after Frederick Joseph Waldo (1852–1936), British physician who studied under Pasteur and Koch. He was a coroner and lecturer as well as an important hygienist, and used metal 'fingers' as clamps in the operating theatre.

(b) Named after Tobjorn Svend Waldo (1927–   ), Swedish developer of the so-called 'bionic' arm. Intended for medical use, the Waldo unit is now used for the handling of radioactive materials.

(c) Named after Waldo Pepper (1896–1929), Boston aviator who lost all his limbs in a salami machine, and suffered from flea bites.

MILD
INSULTS

BATTY
eccentric behaviour

(a) Named after Ivor Battsin de Bellfrie (1851–1926), Welsh miner, who cut coal with his teeth and vice versa.

(b) Named after Miss Batty, the weird schoolmistress in Charles Dickens' *Our Mutual Friend*.

(c) Named after Fitzeherbert Batty (1800–?) a certified lunatic, who was also magistrate of Spanish Town, Jamaica.

BERK
Fool, watered-down meaning from Cockney rhyming slang, 'Berkley Hunt . . .'

(a) Named after Lord Grenville Berkley (1792–1853), Master of the Royal Hunt for over twenty years, who sometimes joined the hounds in ripping up game with his claws and teeth. He liked the livers best.

(b) Named after George Charles Grantly Fitzhardinge Berkley (1800–81), the sixth son of the fifth earl. A notorious huntsman and bully, he nearly killed a publisher named Fraser in whose magazine had appeared a bad review of one of Berkley's rotten novels.

(c) Named after Charles Lemuel Berkley (1861–96), Whig member of parliament, who was quite simply the biggest Berkley Hunt of his day.

BOSIE
googliefied delivery of a cricket ball

(a) Named after B J T Bosanquet (1877–1936), grandfather of newscaster Reginald, when he toured Australia for England in 1903.

(b) Named after Lord Alfred 'Bosie' Douglas (1877–1936), whose cricket balls were greatly loved by Oscar Wilde, and which led to the great man's imprisonment and death.

(c) Named after B O Zee (1877–1936), sports manufacturer of Scrotun, Dumfrieshire. His substandard balls were banned from first class cricket.

BURK
smother, hush up

(a) Named after Henrietta Burk (1829–71), who stifled her infant daughter, and hid her tiny body in an apple tree. The nursery rhyme 'Hush-a-bye-baby' is derived from this macabre case.

(b) Named after William Burk (1792–1829), the Irish partner of William Hare. These two villains executed the infamous Edinburgh murders that supplied subjects for the slab of Dr Robert Knox. Burk smothered his victims. He was hanged in public.

(c) Named after Diego Gordon Burke (1871–1939), the first man to shoot down a Zeppelin, over Harrow-on-the-Weald, in 1917.

COCKY

to be self-confident to the point of being offensive

(a) Named after John George Cockborne DFC (1892–1917), a Scottish pilot who specialized in flying behind enemy lines, and dropping hand-thrown bombs on munitions dumps. He was notorious for taking risks, and was killed trying to fly under the Schelde bridge in Belgium.

(b) Named after Cocky (1795–97), a black fighting cockerel, owned by Edmund Hare of Chatham. Cocky never lost a fight in his rigorous professional career earning Hare a small fortune, which he determinedly drank away.

(c) Named after Edward Cocker (1631–75), a London school-master and the author of *Arithmetik* in 1675. He became a legend in his own lifetime for being a know-all, and insufferably correct.

CUSHY

easy work, idle and undemanding

(a) Named after Cushi, Indian god of sloth, gluttony and self-gratification who is gaining an increasing following in Cornwall. The god demands absolutely nothing of his followers.

(b) Named after Sir Dennis Cushing (1884–1951), philanthropist and faggot manufacturer. His factory was clean, well organized and full of happy faggot-makers who received twice-yearly bonuses and a decorated Christmas faggot.

(c) Named after Cushy (*Old Testament, 2 Samuel 18*). Cushy was entrusted by Jacob to run and tell King David of the death of his son. Ahimag outran the idle Cushy and broke the news of the battle to everyone, but it was Cushy who dawdled into the King to tell him.

DAFFY
befuddled, silly

(a) Named after Daffy Duck, enduring cartoon canard, whose most notable trait is a rasping lisp. Not as cunning or vindictive as his animated cousin Donald, Daffy is more likely to slip on the banana skin than plant it.

(b) Named after Thomas Daffy, seventeenth century Leicestershire clergyman, who concocted the celebrated Daffy's Elixir. Brewed from tincture of senna and stirred with a drop of gin, it was often given to infants, rendering them more than somewhat befuddled.

(c) Named after Henrietta Maria D'Affie (1584–1629). Possibly the most moronic woman ever to attend the Royal Court of France. She was slack-jawed, dull-eyed, incredibly clumsy and prone to thunderous flatulence, but she had a fifty inch bust, for which reason she was tolerated.

DIDDLE
to swindle, to interfere with intimately

(a) Named after Jeremy Diddler in 1803. Diddler was a scrounger and a cheat who caught the public's imagination in J Kenny's stage farce, 'Raising the Wind'.

(b) Named after Tom Diddler in 1853. Diddler was the real name of the young Artful Dodger in Charles Dickens' classic story *Oliver Twist*.

(c) Named after Sir Edward Diddle (1853–1915), unpopular Chancellor of the Exchequer in David Lloyd George's first War cabinet, and the architect of the Purchase Tax System.

GONE FOR A BURTON
met an unfortunate end

(a) Named after Sir Richard Burton (1870–1926), the historian and explorer, who discovered the 'cursed' tomb of Pharoah Rameses II. Within twelve months Burton, his wife, daughter, brother and horse were all dead.

(b) Named after Richard Burton (1926–84). Welsh actor and fodder for gossip columnists. Young ladies seen in his company were tagged to be 'gone on him', a 1950s expression meaning 'smitten'.

(c) Named after Montague Burton the Tailors, whose Blackpool premises were taken over by the RAF in 1939 for training tests. Anyone not accounted for at roll call was said to be having his measurements taken at Burton's.

GUBBINS
stuff and nonsense

(a) Named after Jacob Gubbins (1871–1923). The Gubbins factory produced the webbing straps that were standard issue to the British Forces in the Great War. Backpacks, rifles, blankets, water canteens and all the paraphernalia of war were hung from 'Gubbins'.

(b) Named after Elizabeth Urquart-Gubbins (1923–76), who appeared before King George VI at Royal Ascot in 1949 in a full-length dress made entirely of burnished spam tins.

(c) Named after Nat Gubbins (1893–1976), the humorous columnist on the *Sunday Express* from 1930–53. His wry words brought much needed comic relief to the newspapers during the Second World War.

HOOKY
web of lies, truancy

(a) Named after Captain Hook, the hook-nosed, hook-handed pirate in J M Barry's *Peter Pan*. An enduring and endearing rogue.

(b) Named after William Hookie (1858–1911), Tory M P for Brighton and Hove for over twenty years, during which time he was never known to attend the House of Commons once.

(c) Named after John 'Hooky' Walker, a nineteenth century spy. Walker was a brilliant and inventive liar, with a big, fat putty-coloured nose which bent in a hook attempting to kiss his chin.

NAMBY-PAMBY
effiminate softy

(a) Named after Murli Nambipambi (1832–1900), who ran a homosexual brothel in Poona frequented by British army officers. Nambipambi also changed travellers' cheques providing you had a banker's card.

(b) Named after Ambrose Philips (1675–1749), a member of parliament, a poet, and a judge in Ireland but not England. Philips was given this nickname by Henry Carey because of the wishy-washy poetry that he spewed forth, and for which he was unkindly ridiculed.

(c) Named after Naomi Pambey (1884–1947), stalwart of the Bloomsbury set, who took the whole thing seriously. She wrote the children's story *Andy Pandy*, which involved a male model, a blonde and a bear who lived together in a hinged box.

SCALES AND MEASURES

AMPERE
a unit of electrical current

(a) Named after Amperion the god of air, and son of Apollo the sun god. Amperion made love to Electra in mid-air, thereby planting Icarus in her womb.

(b) Named after André Marie Ampere (1775–1836). Born in Lyons he became a member of the Academy. Ampere wrote the pioneering *Théorie des Phénomènes Electro-Dynamiques* in 1830.

(c) Named after Gustav Adolph Ampere (1836–1900). Born in Brest, Ampere was the first man to fully understand the implications of the ding-dong door chime.

ANGSTROM
unit for measuring the wavelengths of light

(a) Named after Eugene Angstrom (1890–1945), prolific American inventor and mud-wrestling promoter, who first assembled a sundial which was operative twenty-four hours a day.

(b) Named after Angstromidon (365?–302 BC), pupil of Archimedes and nut-tree grower, who stated that light cannot travel through darkness.

(c) Named after Anders Jonas Angstrum (1814–74), Secretary to the Royal Society at Uppsala, Sweden, and tree pruner. He named his son Knut.

ATLAS
book of world maps

(a) Named after Colin Cedric Atlas (1776–1843). An English traveller and cartographer, Atlas produced the first comprehensive collection of maps of the world for his patron, the governor of West Hartlepool.

(b) Named after Atlas the Titan. As a punishment for siding with his Titan pals against Zeus, he was made to hold up the sky, keeping it separate from the Earth. He was resident in north-west Africa, where his mountains still remain.

(c) Named after Charles J Atlas (1911–   ). Tired of being an eight stone weakling and unable to open the fridge, Atlas vowed to transform himself into the strongest man in the world. He only succeeded in building up his ears, but earns a modest living modelling deaf aids.

BEAUFORT SCALE
graded wind speeds

(a) Named after Beofor, Danish god of seas and storms, whose terrible anger could be appeased by throwing a Viking sailor over the side.

(b) Named after Rear Admiral Sir Francis Beaufort (1774–1857). The son of a clergyman, he entered the Royal Navy at the age of thirteen and was appointed admiral as an old man of seventy-two. Beaufort was hydrographer to the navy for twenty-six years.

(c) Named after Jean-Claude Beaufort (1691–1767). The son of a Paris baker, he invented a system of judging wind speed by counting the revolutions of a wind-blown paper wheel.

CELSIUS
scale for measurement of temperature

(a) Named after Anders Celsius (1701–44), a Swedish astronomer and inventor of the centigrade thermometer. Celsius decided that water freezes at zero degrees and boils at one hundred degrees.

(b) Named after Alka Celsia (1804–82), a Hungarian cook who devised the 'regulo' grading system of oven temperature control.

(c) Named after Celsiu Agricolus Felatium (AD 216–170), mystic and alchemist, who stated that water boils at one hundred degrees and freezes at zero degrees.

FAHRENHEIT
scale of temperature

(a) Named after Gabriel Daniel Fahrenheit (1686–1736), German physicist living in England, who also founded modern meteorology and built a successful hydrometer.

(b) Named after Linda Fahren (1786–1836), who was blessed with the skill of spontaneously breaking wind whenever the temperature fell to thirty-two degrees.

(c) Named after Fahrenheit Faure Fyveone (1886–1936), Sino-Welsh weather forecaster for Radio Stockholm, until his accident.

GEIGER COUNTER
instrument for measuring radioactivity

(a) Named after Marie Jutten Geiger (1901–42), student of Albert Einstein. She invented the instrument in 1933, dying of leukaemia as a direct result of her work.

(b) Named after Monty Geiger (1924–   ), the celebrated Isle of Wight ventriloquist and nuclear physicist. Mr Geiger has the ability to glow in the dark.

(c) Named after Hans Wilhelm Geiger (1882–1945). Born at Neustadt-an-der-Hardt, Geiger worked with Rutherford on splitting the atom. He constructed his counter in 1911.

HERTZ
wireless wavelength

(a) Named after Klaus Walter Hertz (1872–1939). Disillusioned with his research into wireless transmission, Hertz sold out to Marconi in 1909 and went into the rent-a-car business.

(b) Named after Heinrich Rudolph Hertz (1857–94). Hertz was a professor of physics at Karlsruhe. His research was of great importance, and it can be said that he founded the basis of all modern radio theory.

(c) Named after Helmholtz Hertz (1863–1948). Having pioneered wireless telegraphy in Germany, Hertz was made honorary doctor of science at Leipzig. A victim of Nazi persecution, he fled to London and died in despair after listening to the first episode of 'The Archers', on the BBC Home Service.

JOULE
electrical unit

(a) Named after Joule Verne (1821–98), the French fantasy adventure writer. In his book *Around the World in Eighty days* Verne accurately described a formula relating to heat, current, time and units of electricity. Verne also prophesied interplanetary travel, giant submarines and war planes.

(b) Named after James Prescott Joule (1818–89), Salford-born Fellow of the Royal Society who proved that heat is a form of energy.

(c) Named after Joule B Saurry (1812–1914), the Belgian inventor of the dynamo, the electric slot-meter and electric toilet paper wiper.

MACH NUMBER
ratio of the speed of an object compared with the local speed of sound

(a) Named after Ernest Mach (1838–1916), a brilliant Austrian philosopher of science and phenomenology. He taught young Albert Einstein a thing or two.

(b) Named after Max Mach (1839–1942), German rocketeer and father of the modern missile. He taught young Werner von Braun a thing or two.

(c) Named after Hans Gonzales 'Dirty' Mach (1906–58), Swiss mathematician who emigrated to Brazil. Mach mounted the legendary Temporal-Polar experiment, wherein he ran around the South Pole, against the rotation of the Earth, and travelled backwards in time.

OHM
unit of electrical resistance

(a) Named after Oliver Henry Morse (1790–1871), who used his initials only when presenting his papers to the Royal Society. He invented the rheostat and postulated the construction of a fuse mechanism, which he called a 'Safety Chasm'.

(b) Named after Georg Simon Ohm (1787–1854), German physicist. The multitalented Ohm undertook important research in the fields of maths, accoustics and crystals, as well as electricity.

(c) Named after Ohm, the mystic's god of meditation. Devotees normally sit cross-legged slowly intoning his name, until they offer no resistance and can be pushed over by small children without difficulty.

ORRERY
clockwork device demonstrating the relative movements of the solar system

(a) Named after Denys O'Rery (1714–80). Unable to read a map, O'Rery navigated the streets of Dublin by stars at night, and by his star-machine by day. It weighed several hundredweight, and he pushed it about in a hand cart.

(b) Named after Charles Boyle, Fourth Earl of Orrery (1676–1731), by its inventor George Graham, who was a toady.

(c) Named after Aurora, Roman goddess of the night sky, who mothered four thousand and twelve children, each one a little shining star.

PLIMSOLL LINE
mandatory marking on the hull of a ship, indicating safe-loading levels

(a) Named after Isaac Dockers Plimsoll (1847–1923), Secretary of State for Transport and Shipping in the Mac-Donald Cabinet. Plimsoll ran a tight ship, inheriting the Isle of Thanet ferry from his godfather, Earl Bostik.

(b) Named after Bunyun Korn, Second Swetti of Plimsoll (1837–1901), inventor of the running shoe, sufferer from running sores and composer of 'The Road to Mandalay.'

(c) Named after Samuel Plimsoll (1824–98), known in some circles as 'the sailor's friend'. An English social reformer, his Line was adopted in 1876. Plimsoll was the author of *Cattle Ships* in 1890, railing against the cruelty of on-the-hoof cattle exporting, which persists to this day.

RICHTER SCALE
measurement of the intensity of earthquakes

(a) Named after Rhichta, the Cheyenne god of earthquakes. The Californian Indian population correctly predicted the massive San Franscisco earthquake in 1906.

(b) Named after Charles Francis Richter (1900–), professor of seismology at the Californian Institute of Technology. The scale was first proposed by the German Dr Bruno Gutenburg.

(c) Named after Rick Tar, the grossly overweight whaling captain in Milton's tragic poem 'Blubber'.

VERNIER
movable scale for obtaining tiny measurements

(a) Named after Gordon Bleu Vernier (1792–1865), famed Marseilles chef, who spent the major part of his life trying to formulate exact ratios for the ingredients of eel sausage.

(b) Named after Henry Montrose, Third Duke of Vernier (1811–58). Suspicious of his servants, Vernier invented an invisible method of marking wine bottles, to see if the contents were being secretly filched.

(c) Named after Pierre Vernier (1580–1637), the French mathematician who invented the scale in 1631, and published *Le Quadrant Nouveau de Mathematiques*.

VOLT
electrical unit of current

(a) Named after Voltaire (1694–1778), friend of Frederick the Great and Madame de Pompadour, indifferent historian, Bastille prisoner and a man with an electric wit.

(b) Named after John Travolta (1872–1951). The son of a Welsh miner, Travolta invented the first commercially viable dry battery cell. He was also an eccentric dancer at weddings.

(c) Named after Count Alessandro Volta (1745–1827), the Italian physicist who in 1775 produced electric charges by induction. By 1800 he had developed voltaic piles.

WATT
unit of electrical power or activity

(a) Named after Sir Walter Watt (1772–1841), Dundee landlord and poet, who invented the coin-in-the-slot electricity meter in 1837.

(b) Named after Do Watt (1819–1900), the deaf inventor and a great worry to his mother, who constructed a household kettle after being inspired by the sight of a reciprocating steam engine.

(c) Named after James Watt (1736–1819), the Scottish inventor and mechanical engineer, who conceived of and constructed the first modern condensing steam engine in 1765.

NATURAL
PHENOMENA

ECHO
distant voice, repeating original sounds

(a) Named after Echo, a nymph from Mount Helicon. As a punishment for helping Zeus to fornicate with all the other little nymphs, she was unable to begin any conversation, but could only repeat the words of others. Spurned by Narcissus she pined and faded away until only her voice was left.

(b) Named after David Echo (1966–), the inventor of a bakelite (*qv*) art deco wireless set, which runs on margarine.

(c) Named after Echo, one of the three Muses. She was empowered to endow poets with creative thought. A hopeless task, she transformed herself into a whisper, but failing to make herself heard above the traffic she became a blood-red jewel, and was eaten by a small weasel.

ELECTRICITY
natural spontaneous power source

(a) Named after Electra, the daughter of Atlas. She was kidnapped and carried off to Mount Olympus, and is now a dim or invisible star, consumed by grief.

(b) Named after Barthelov Electrus (1362–1420), the Milanese alchemist and philosopher. Electrus suggested that all primal power was delivered from the heavens to the earth by means of a force. He saw this as an invisible chain of links which he called 'electrons'.

(c) Named after Electrion, the Roman god of lightning. Father of Romulus, mother of Remus, and good friends with the Schwartzes.

FORTUNE
luck or chance, great wealth

(a) Named after the Roman goddess Fortuna, who brought her worshippers good luck and prosperity.

(b) Named after Enrico Llewellyn Fortuno (1317–1420). Due to the earliest recorded printing error legend has it that everything he touched turned into golf.

(c) Named after King Fortunus, sometimes known as King Midas, the father of Croesus.

HELIUM
gaseous element

(a) Named after Helios, macho son of Hyperion, giver of life and Greek god.

(b) Named after Professor Ramsay Heliot (1872–1951) of Aberdeen, revitaliser of the airship industry after the disasters of the 1930s involving the hydrogen filled Hindenburg and R101.

(c) Named after Flatulus Helium (97–50 BC), Roman Senator and embarrassing dinner guest.

NEMESIS
massive come-uppance

(a) Named after Nemesis II (813–762 BC), Egyptian king who was closely associated with the sun god Ra. Nemesis was an authoritarian sadist, his enemies were humiliated and buried alive, as were his friends. In legend it was this king who reduced great tracts of his country to desert.

(b) Named after Antoine Nemesse (1715–61). The original 'Mad Axeman', Nemesse was a public executioner, over-active in Montpelier. He took over twenty blows to decapitate a youth convicted of sheep stealing. Nemesse happened to be the Mayor's son.

(c) Named after Nemesis, the goddess of retribution for evil deeds and undeserved good fortune. Nemesis transformed herself into a snow white goose in order to escape rape by Zeus. However, Zeus became a swan and raped her. The outcome of this union was a splendid egg, which hatched into the beautiful Helen.

ST ELMO'S FIRE
blue ionic glow or discharge, usually from thunderclouds, as seen around ships' masts

(a) Named after St Erasmus, patron saint of Mediterranean sailors.

(b) Named after Elmer Gantry (1701–76), who disappeared in a blue flash while being hung from the yard-arm.

(c) Named after St Elmo, patron saint of Lithuanian lamp-lighters.

SILHOUETTE
an outline, or shadow portrait

(a) Named after Antoine Silhouette (1807–60), the totally hairless, heavily carbuncled bore, whose hideous profile looked the same no matter which way up he wore his head.

(b) Named after Etienne de Silhouette (1709–67), Comptroller General of France, appointed to his office through the influence of Madame de Pompadour. He was ridiculed for his loony ideas, namely seeing everything in terms of black and white, and was forced to resign after one chaotic year.

(c) Named after Fournaud Silhouette (1752–98), pioneer journalist who was active in Paris. He included facsimile portraits of celebrities in his pamphlets, showing only their outlines, which he traced from shadows.

GENTLE EXPLETIVES

BLIMEY O'REILLY!
mild expletive

(a) Named after Blind O'Reilly, a Liverpool docker. O'Reilly rose to prominence in the late nineteenth century as an active trade unionist.

(b) Named after Patrick John O'Reilly (1813–65), who became greatly moved during a church sermon whose text was, 'If thine eyes offend thee, pluck them out'. He did.

(c) Named after Old Mother Reilly, alias Arthur Lucan (1887–1954), whose wife Kitty McShane played his stage daughter. The phrase came into common usage in 1937 as the result of the catchphrase in their first film.

CODSWALLOP!
nonsense

(a) Named after Hiram Codd in 1870, when he designed a bottle which kept beer or 'wallop' fresh, by means of its own gas pressure holding a marble tightly against the neck.

(b) Named after Sir Percival 'Codswallop' Trusse (1319–82), whose main occupation appears to have been kicking gentlemen in the codpiece.

(c) Named after Frank Kadzvalop (1861–1937), American vaudeville artist, who specialized in nonsense songs, accompanied by his ukelele.

CRAP
excreted waste matter

(a) Named after Lodovol Crapski (1947–), scriptwriter to Benny Hill.

(b) Named after Thomas Crapper of Doncaster, inventor in 1837 of the first flushing toilet, 'Crapper's Valveless Water Waste Preventor'.

(c) Named after Sir Christopher Crap (1837–1947), an incompetent lawyer who sometimes fulfilled his briefs.

GEE WHIZZ!
exclamation of surprise

(a) Named after G Barratt Witz (1851–1923), the candy baron of Essex. His famous Sherbert Dab was sold under the slogan 'G Witz! Sweet Perfection!'

(b) Named after Jesus Christ (0–33), Jewish revolutionary and son of God. A euphemism for the blasphemous use of the name 'Je-sus!'

(c) Named after Dgheewas, the Tamil god of unforeseen events. The British army stationed in Bombay adopted his name as a reaction to military cock-ups.

GORDON BENNETT!
mild expletive

(a) Named after James Gordon Bennett (1841–1918), the son of the founder of the *New York Herald*, instigator of the Gordon Bennett Cup, and the man who commissioned Stanley to go and search for Dr Livingstone in the jungle, because he thought it would sell newspapers.

(b) Named after Gordon James Bennett (1841–1918), the Hampshire eccentric, who unsuccessfully attempted to cross the English Channel by various means, including bathtub, tightrope and swing doors. Bennett was drowned several times before giving up.

(c) Named after Gordon J G Bennett (1841–1918), the son of the founder of the *Hampshire Chronicle*, and the man who offered a prize of £100 to the first man to swim the English Channel.

GREAT SCOTT!
good heavens!

(a) Named after Robert Falcon Scott (1868–1912), the English explorer who led the National Antarctic Expedition of 1901, and the second tragic Expedition of 1910 from which only his diaries survived.

(b) Named after General Winfield Scott, a former soldier who tried, but failed, to become President of the United States.

(c) Named after J G Scott (?–1884), an American giant who was exhibited as the 'World's Strongest Man' in New York. Over seven feet tall, and weighing thirty-six stone, Scott's body was bequeathed to science, and his skeleton may be seen in the Guggenheim Museum.

LIKE BILLIO!
enthusiastically

(a) Named after Captain Billio, the 1950s children's cinema space hero. The good captain would blast off weekly to save the world with the cry, 'Fight the foe . . . like Billio!'

(b) Named after Joseph Billio, founder of the Independent Congregation in 1682 at Maldon in Essex. Zealot, proselytiser, insomniac, celibate and priest.

(c) Named after William O Cody (1811–77), alias Buffalo Bill, alias 'Billy O'. His energetic and spectacular wild west shows numbed three continents to the library.

OK!
expression of approval

(a) Named after Old Keokuk, an American Indian chief, who signed all treaties with the treacherous white-man, using his initials.

(b) Named after O K Sahnewurst (1873–1944), the originator of a spicy brown sauce marketed under the slogan, 'If it tastes good, it's OK.'

(c) Named after O K D'Euquai (1821–1909), the pioneer of the 'champagne' method of producing sparkling white wine. Until 1940, it was still a capital offence in France to sell fake champagne that was not 'OK'.

NATTY!
dapper, slickly dressed

(a) Named after Nat Gonella (1917–), British jazz trumpeter, whose popularity has survived over a long musical career. Nat wore his Brylcreem and tuxedo with the best of them.

(b) Named after Natty Dread, Rasta deity of Jamaica, for whose sake his followers go to extraordinary trouble in hiring oiled clothes from Moss Bros for ceremonial ten pin bowling.

(c) Named after Jean Nattier (1685–1766), French portrait painter of the wealthy and the famous and the richly dressed, including Peter the Great. He also gave his name to the colour Nattier Blue.

SWEET FANNY ADAMS!
Nothing at all. (Also 'sweet FA!')

(a) Named after Francis Adams (1867–1917), Hampshire sweet manufacturer and inventor of the gobstopper, a multi-layered ball of sugar that provided lengthy sucking until all that was left was the paper wrapper.

(b) Named after Fanny Adams (1859–67) murdered and chopped into small pieces by William Baker, a solicitor's clerk. The gruesome killing coincided with the introduction of tinned meat in the Royal Navy, and the phrase was coined by Portsmouth sailors.

(c) Named after Frances Adams (1867–1937), wife of Henry Adams, the first chairman of the Football Association. She was a notorious coquette, but was never known to be unfaithful to her husband.

THE REAL McCOY!
the genuine article

(a) Named after Graham Alexis McCoy (1850–90), British jeweller and inventor, who subdivided the Koh I Noor diamond into its feeble diminutions, and invented the allegoric lie-detector, utilizing his sweat-rheostat.

(b) Named after Alice Marie MacCoy (1854–1906), a New Zealand orphan who was brought to Aberdeen in 1874 by Hugh Innes, as claimant to a fortune. MacCoy inherited successfully but married unwisely, being murdered by her husband . . . Hugh Innes.

(c) Named after Captain William McCoy, a bankrupt in 1919, but a millionaire by 1925, thanks to whisky smuggling during Prohibition. The captain would anchor his boat off the coast of Florida and his customers rowed out for a crate or two of booze.

ANSWERS

Achilles Heel (b)
Adam's Apple (a)
Adonis (a)
Albert (b)
Alice Springs (a)
America (c)
Ampere (b)
Anderson Shelter (a)
Angstrom (c)
Atlas (b)
August (c)
Aunt Sally (c)

Bakelite (a)
Batty (c)
Beaufort Scale (b)
Begonia (b)
Belcher (c)
Belisha Beacon (c)
Berk (b)
Big Ben (c)
Big Bertha (a)
Birdseye (a)
Biro (a)
Black Maria (a), (b), (c)
Blanket (a)
Blimey O'Reilly (a)
Bloody Mary (b)
Bloomers (c)
Bluchers (a)
Bluebeard (a)
Bobby (b)
Boffin (a)
Bosie (a)
Bowdlerize (b)
Bowie (a)
Bowler (a)
Boycott (c)

Bunsen Burner (a)
Braille (a)
Bramah Lock (a)
Burk (b)
Burnham Scale (c)
Busby (a)

Cabal (c)
Caesarean (b)
Calypso (a)
Cant (c)
Cardigan (a)
Casanova (c)
Catherine Wheel (a)
Celsius (a)
Chauvinist (b)
Chesterfield (c)
Chippendale (c)
Christy Minstrel (b)
Chrysler (a)
Chubb Lock (c)
Cissy (c)
Clerihew (a)
Cocky (c)
Codswallop (a)
Colt 45 (b)
Condom (a)
Coty (c)
Crap (b)
Crapps (a)
Crufts (a)
Cushy (c)

Daffy (b)
Dahlia (a)
Davenport (b)
Davy Lamp (b)
Delaware (b)

Demijohn (a)
Derrick (c)
Derringer (b)
Diddle (a)
Diesel (c)
Dixieland (b)
Dobro (c)
Doily (c)
Doubting Thomas (b)
Draconian (a)
Dunce (c)

Echo (a)
Electricity (a)
Epicurean (b)
Erotic (b)
Everest (b)

Fabian (c)
Fahrenheit (a)
Fallopian Tubes (c)
Ferris Wheel (c)
Flora and Fauna (b)
Fokker (c)
Fortune (a)
Friday (c)
Frisbee (a)
Fuschia (b)

Galvanize (c)
Gamp (b)
Gardenia (a)
Gargantuan (a)
Gat (a)
Gee Whizz (b)
Geiger Counter (c)
Georgette (b)
Gerrymander (c)
Gillette (a)
Goliath (c)
Gone for a Burton (c)
Goon (a)
Gordon Bennett (a)
Granny Smith (a)

Great Scott (b)
Greengage (c)
Grimsby (b)
Grog, Groggy (c)
Gubbins (c)
Guillotine (c)
Guppy (b)

Ham (a)
Hansom (a)
Helium (a)
Hercules (b)
Hermaphrodite (c)
Hertz (b)
Hilton (a)
Hippocratic Oath (a)
Hobson's Choice (a)
Hooker (a)
Hooky (c)
Hooligan (a)
Hoover (a)
Houdini (a)
Hygiene (a)
Hypnotism (c)

Iris (b)

Jack Johnson (c)
Jack Russell (a)
Jaegers (a)
January (b)
Jeroboam (a)
Jezebel (c)
John Paul Jones (b)
Jonah (c)
Joule (b)
Juggernaut (b)
Jumbo (c)
Jupiter (a)

Kelvinator (a)
Kilroy Was Here (a)
Knickers (c)

Leotard (b)
Lesbian (a)
Lewis Gun (b)
Like Billio (b)
Limerick (b)
Listerine (c)
Lobelia (c)
Loganberry (c)
Lucifer (b)
Luddite (c)
Lunatic (b)
Lush (a)
Lynch Law (a)

Mach Number (a)
Macintosh (b)
Mae West (a)
Maginot Line (b)
Magpie (b)
Malapropism (c)
Mansard (c)
March (b)
Mars (b)
Martinet (c)
Marxism (c)
Masochist (a)
Mata Hari (b)
Maudlin (c)
Mauser (a)
Maverick (b)
Melba (a)
Mercury (c)
Mesmerist (c)
Mickey Finn (c)
Mills Bomb (b)
Molotov Cocktail (b)
Money (b)
Monkey Wrench (b)
Moonie (b)
Morse Code (b)
Mumbo Jumbo (a)

Namby Pamby (b)
Narcissus (a)

Natty (c)
Nemesis (c)
Neptune (c)
Nicotine (c)
Nosey Parker (a)

Ohm (b)
O K (a)
Onanist (c)
Orrery (b)
Oscar (b)

Panic (c)
Pasteurize (c)
Pavlova (c)
Peeler (a)
Peeping Tom (b)
Pennsylvania (c)
Peter Stuyvesant (c)
Phaeton (a)
Pinchbeck (b)
Pinkerton (a)
Platonic Love (b)
Plimsoll Line (c)
Pluto (c)
Poe (c)
Poinsettia (a)
Pompadour (b)
Pry (c)
Puff (b)
Puffing Billy (b)
Pullman (c)
Python (a)
Pyrrhic Victory (c)

Quisling (b)

Rachmanism (c)
Raglan (a)
Renault (b)
Reuters (b)
Rhodesia (b)
Richter Scale (b)
Ritz (c)

Sadism (b)
St Elmo's Fire (a)
St Leger (c)
Saint Vitus Dance (b)
Sam Browne (a)
Sandwich (c)
Santa Claus (b)
Saturday (b)
Saturn (a)
Saxophone (a)
Scrooge (b)
Shrapnel (c)
Sheraton (a)
Shyster (a)
Sideburns (a)
Silhouette (b)
Silly Billy (b)
Sousaphone (c)
Spartacist (b)
Spode (b)
Spoonerism (a)
Stentorian (a)
Stetson (b)
Sweet Fanny Adams (b)

Taciturn (c)
Tam O'Shanter (b)
Tantalize (b)
Tarmac (a)
Tasmania (b)
Taxi (b)
Teddy Bear (c)
Teddy Boy (a)
The Real McCoy (c)
Thespian (c)

Thursday (b)
Tich (a)
Tom Collins (a)
Tommy Gun (c)
Tontine (c)
Trilby (a)
Tristan Da Cunha (a)
Trollop (b)
Tupperware (b)
Tureen (a)

Union Jack (b)
Uranus (a)

Vancouver (a)
Venus (c)
Vernier (c)
Very Light (c)
Vesta (b)
Volt (c)
Vulcanize (b)

Waldo (a)
Watt (c)
Wedgwood (a)
Wednesday (b)
Wellington Boot (c)
Wisteria (a)
Woolworths (b)

Xenophobic (b)

Zeppelin (b)
Ziegfeld Girl (c)
Zinnia (c)